CONTEN

1 CHARACTERISTICS OF LIVING ORGANISMS

1 Nutrition – obtaining energy and materials needed for life.
2 Respiration – transfer of energy from 'energy rich' materials, e.g. carbohydrates and fats, to a usable form (ATP).
3 Growth – ability to increase in size and/or complexity.
4 Excretion – removal of harmful wastes produced by the body.
5 Sensitivity – detection of stimuli from the environment.
6 Movement – plants move parts, e.g. leaves move to face the sun; animals move parts but can also typically move from place to place (locomotion).
7 Reproduction – ability to produce offspring.

Levels of organization

1 **Cells** are made up of complex interactions of chemicals.
2 **Tissues** are made up of a number of similar cells acting together, e.g. connective tissue.
3 **Organs** are made up of a number of different tissues acting together, e.g. liver.

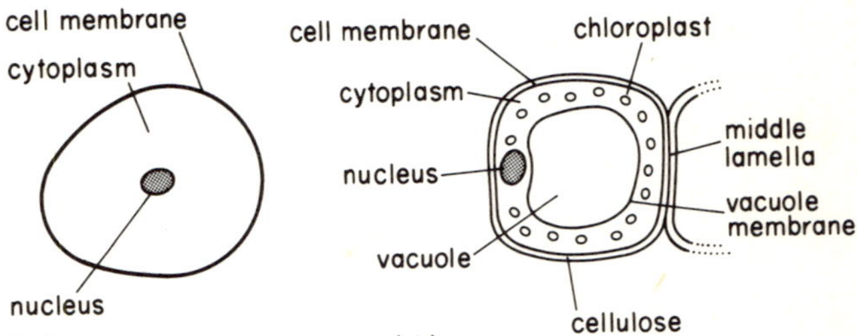

Fig. 1.1 *(a) Animal cell. (b) Plant cell under light microscope.*

4 **Systems** are made up of organs acting together, e.g. digestive system.

The cell

The cell is the basic unit of life. Many organisms consist of only a single cell, e.g. *Amoeba*, yeast; others are multicellular, consisting of many cells. There are many different types of cells, each with certain special features; however, all animal cells show similarities, all plant cells show similarities, and all cells (both plant and animal) have certain features in common.

Some features common to all cells

1 **Nucleus** – control centre of the cell. Contains the hereditary material.
2 **Cytoplasm** – substance of all living cells. Carries out all the chemical reactions necessary for life.
3 **Cell membrane** (plasmalemma) – membrane surrounding the cytoplasm. It is semipermeable, allowing water to pass more easily than many dissolved substances. It also actively controls the entry and exit of many substances.
4 **Mitochondria** – specialized organelles in the cytoplasm, the centres of aerobic **respiration** in the cell, found in large numbers in cells requiring much energy.
5 **Endoplasmic reticulum** – membrane-lined canals and cavities, thought to be involved with the transport and storage of materials in the cell.
6 **Ribosomes** – tiny granules in the cytoplasm, some attached to the membranes of the endoplasmic reticulum. Centres of protein synthesis.

Some features common only to plant cells

1 **Cell wall** – composed of **cellulose** fibres, elastic, allowing the cell to change its volume slightly. Provides shape, support and protection. It is fully permeable to all dissolved substances.
2 **Chloroplastids** – found only in green plant tissues, contain the green pigment **chlorophyll**. Centres of **photosynthesis**.
3 **Vacuole** – large central fluid-filled cavity in the cytoplasm surrounded by a membrane and containing vacuolar sap.

Differences between animal cells and plant cells

Animal	*Plant*
Cell membrane only	Cell membrane and cellulose wall
No large central vacuole	Large central vacuole
No chloroplastids	Chloroplastids in green tissues
No chlorophyll	Chlorophyll in chloroplastids
No middle lamella	Cells joined by middle lamella
Carbohydrate stored as glycogen	Carbohydrate stored as starch

2 DIFFUSION AND OSMOSIS

Diffusion

1 Diffusion is the movement of substances, either as gases or in solution, from regions of high to regions of low concentration.

2 If uninterrupted it will continue until the substance is evenly distributed in equal concentration.

3 The greater the diffusion gradient, i.e. the greater the difference in concentration between the two regions, the more substance will diffuse.

4 The rate of diffusion increases with temperature.

5 Substances that diffuse into and out of cells are usually in solution.

6 Diffusion is one of the main ways substances move into, out of and between cells and their surroundings, e.g.:

- ⋆ uptake of oxygen and elimination of carbon dioxide at lungs, gills and other respiratory surfaces;
- ⋆ exchange of oxygen and carbon dioxide between blood and tissues;
- ⋆ uptake of end-products of digestion from gut into blood;
- ⋆ uptake of carbon dioxide by leaf cells for photosynthesis.

Osmosis

1 Osmosis is movement of water from a weaker (more dilute, **hypotonic**) to a stronger (more concentrated, **hypertonic**) solution, across a **semipermeable membrane** (one allowing water to pass more rapidly than dissolved substances).

2 If uninterrupted it will continue until the solutions on either side of the membrane are of equal concentration (**isotonic**).

3 The amount of water moved by osmosis increases with increasing concentration difference between solutions.

4 The rate of osmosis increases with temperature.

5 Osmosis is the only way water moves across the cell membrane.

6 If something acts to stop water moving into a solution, an **osmotic pressure** develops as the water pushes against the resistance.

Osmosis in living organisms

If cell contents are at higher concentration than surrounding solution, water will pass across semipermeable cell membrane and enter cell by **endosmosis**. If cell contents are at lower concentration than surrounding solution, water leaves cell by **exosmosis**.

Plant cells

If water enters a plant cell by osmosis the cell increases in volume, the contents exert a pressure on the cell membrane and surrounding cell wall and the cell becomes 'firm' or **turgid**. Water continues to enter the cell until the cell wall can stretch no more. Now **wall pressure** equals the pressure of the incoming water (**osmotic pressure**) and no water can enter.

If water leaves a plant cell by osmosis the cell contents decrease in volume, the pressure against the cell wall decreases and the cell loses its turgidity and becomes 'soft' or **flaccid**. Turgidity is very important in the support of non-woody plant tissues, e.g. leaves; when cells are flaccid the leaves will droop or **wilt**.

If water continues to leave the cell, the cytoplasm eventually starts pulling away from cell wall and the cell is **plasmolysed**.

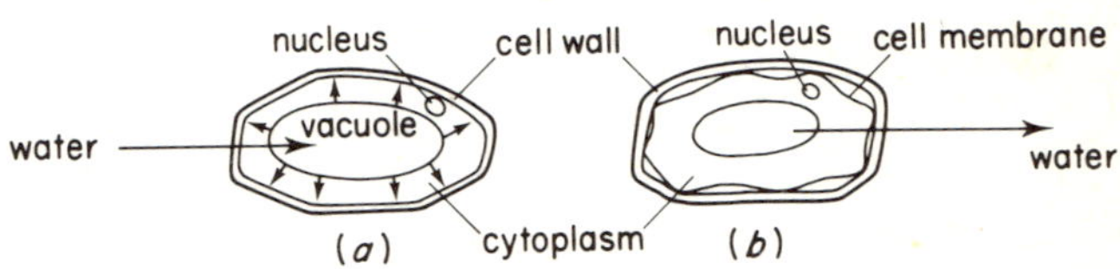

Fig. 2.1 *(a) Turgid, (b) flaccid plasmolysed plant cell*

Animal cells

Animal cells do not have the rigid cell wall that plant cells have; if water enters by osmosis there is the danger that the cell will increase in volume and eventually burst the cell membrane. Therefore animal cells must either be in osmotic equilibrium with surroundings of same concentration as cytoplasm, or **osmoregulate** – actively control amount of water that enters or leaves.

Osmoregulation in animals

Generally the cells of sea-dwelling (marine) invertebrates, e.g. jellyfish, crustacea, etc., are isotonic to seawater so that they are in osmotic equilibrium with their surroundings. However, cells and body fluids (blood) of marine vertebrates, e.g. fish, are much more dilute (hypotonic) than seawater. Therefore they always tend to lose water by osmosis; although surrounded by water, they live in conditions of 'physiological drought'. (For the same reason, we cannot drink seawater as it is more concentrated than our blood and water moves by osmosis from the blood into the seawater in the gut, creating more thirst.) Marine fish have a method of drinking seawater and getting rid of salts.

Freshwater vertebrates are hypertonic to freshwater and continually take up water by osmosis. They must therefore remove this water by producing large volumes of dilute urine.

Experiment to demonstrate osmosis

1 Peel a potato and cut nine narrow strips of tissue of equal dimensions (about 5 cm long).
2 Divide the strips into three groups of three and calculate the average length of strip for each group.
3 Place each group of strips in a separate dish or beaker labelled A, B and C, and completely cover with: A – water; B – 0.3 molar sucrose solution; C – 1.0 molar sucrose solution.
4 Leave the strips in the solutions for about 30 minutes.
5 Remove strips, re-measure lengths, calculate averages.
6 **Expected results:**
   - **A** – strips increase in length, weight, turgidity;
   - **B** – strips remain about same length, weight, turgidity;
   - **C** – strips decrease in length, weight, turgidity.
7 **Explanation:**
   - **A** – water is hypotonic to potato tissue so the strips gain water by osmosis and increase in size;
   - **B** – 0.3 molar sucrose solution is isotonic to potato tissue so the strips neither gain nor lose water by osmosis;
   - **C** – 1.0 molar sucrose solution is hypertonic to potato tissue so the strips lose water by osmosis and shrink.

3 NUTRITION

Living organisms are made up of organic and inorganic substances; they must obtain a supply of these to grow and maintain life. They also require an energy supply to fuel all the life processes. **Organic compounds** are complex carbon-containing compounds such as carbohydrates, fats, proteins and vitamins. **Inorganic compounds** are simpler materials such as mineral salts, water, etc.

Different types of nutrition

1 **Autotrophs** only require simple inorganic compounds, from which they can synthesize all their organic compounds. To do this they need energy.

   ⋆ **Photosynthetic** autotrophs (green plants) obtain their energy from light (under natural conditions the sun), which is absorbed by the green pigment **chlorophyll**. This energy is used to synthesize organic compounds from simple inorganic compounds during the process of **photosynthesis**. Plants that carry out photosynthesis are also called **holophytic**.

   ⋆ **Chemosynthetic** autotrophs (some bacteria) obtain their energy from inorganic chemical reactions that give out energy (**exothermic**). Important in the nitrogen cycle.

2 **Heterotrophs** cannot carry out photosynthesis or chemosynthesis, so require organic and inorganic compounds in their food. These organic compounds come from photosynthetic plants, either directly or indirectly via food chains. Thus all plants and animals are dependent on energy from the sun.

   ⋆ **Holozoic** heterotrophs (*most* animals) swallow organic food.

   ⋆ **Parasitic** heterotrophs (*some* animals and *some* plants, e.g. fungi. Bacteria, and *all* viruses) live and feed on or in a living host.

   ⋆ **Saprophytic** heterotrophs (most fungi and bacteria) live and feed on or in dead organic matter. They are decomposers, of great importance in the recycling of materials in nature.

Holophytic nutrition in green plants

Plants that contain the green pigment chlorophyll carry out photosynthesis in the light. In photosynthesis, complex organic compounds such as sugars and starch are synthesized from carbon dioxide and water:

$$\underset{\text{Carbon dioxide}}{6CO_2} + \underset{\text{Water}}{6H_2O} \xrightarrow[\text{Chlorophyll Enzymes}]{\text{Light}} \underset{\text{Glucose}}{C_6H_{12}O_6} + \underset{\text{Oxygen}}{6O_2}$$

Mineral salts are also required for metabolism and combination into complex organic compounds, e.g. proteins, pigments, ATP, etc. Photosynthesis is the only source of organic compounds (apart from the minor production of chemosynthesis) and oxygen in the air.

The leaf as a photosynthetic structure

1 The broad, flat shape presents large surface area for absorption of sunlight. Arranged to receive maximum light; leaf stalks can bend so leaves are at right-angles to light rays.
2 The thinness of the leaf means that light and carbon dioxide can penetrate rapidly to all cells.
3 The main vein and network of vascular tissue help support the large surface area, and transport water and mineral salts to the photosynthetic cells and sugars away from them.
4 Pores or **stomata**, mainly on lower surface, for uptake of carbon dioxide by diffusion. Water vapour and oxygen leave leaf through stomata – usually open in light, close at night.

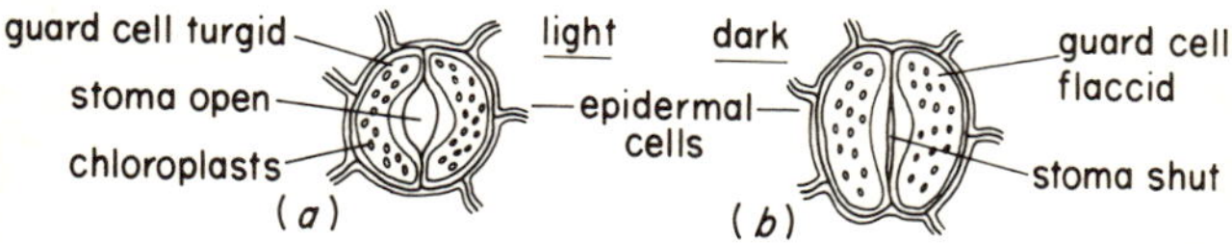

Fig. 3.1 *Stoma (a) open (b) shut*

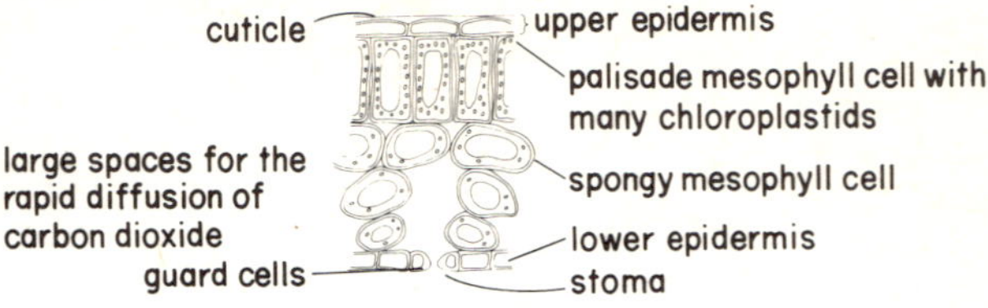

Fig. 3.2 *Typical leaf under light microscope*

Conditions necessary for photosynthesis

1 **Carbon dioxide** diffuses into the leaf through open stomata, via large intercellular spaces of the spongy mesophyll, and dissolves in the surface film of water on palisade mesophyll cells. It diffuses in solution through cell walls, cell membranes and cytoplasm, into chloroplastids (contain chlorophyll and are centres of photosynthesis). As carbon dioxide is used, concentration gradient between chloroplastids and the outside air increases, more carbon dioxide diffuses in.

2 **Water** is absorbed from the soil by **osmosis** by the root hairs of young roots. It passes by osmosis from cell to cell, eventually entering the water-conducting xylem tissue in the centre of the root. It is moved up the stem by the **transpiration stream** to the veins of the leaf. It then moves by osmosis into the leaf cells and reaches the chloroplastids.

3 **Chlorophyll** absorbs light energy, mainly at the red and blue end of the spectrum, reflecting green light.

4 **Light.**

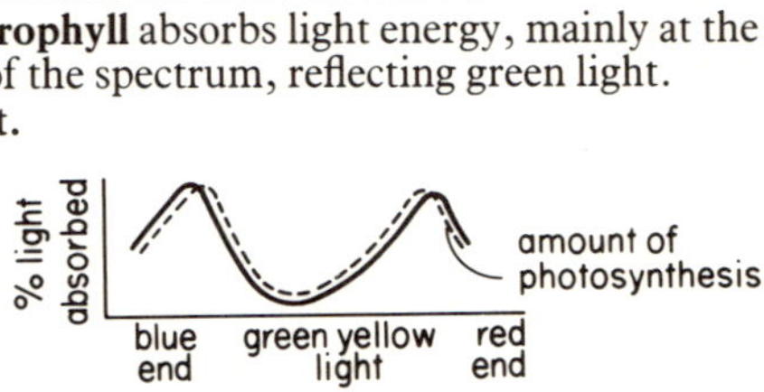

Fig. 3.3 *Photosynthesis and light absorbed*

5 All reactions are catalyzed by **enzymes**.
6 A suitable **temperature** necessary for the enzyme-controlled reactions of photosynthesis.
7 **Mineral salts**.

Products of photosynthesis

1 Simple **sugars**, e.g. glucose, which may be:
  * used as a **source of energy** in respiration;
  * converted to **sucrose** for transport to other parts of plant;
  * converted to **insoluble food storage materials** – starch, fats or oils;
  * converted to **cellulose** fibres for plant cell wall.

2 **Amino acids** and then proteins which form the basis of cytoplasm, including all enzymes.

The process of photosynthesis

The simple equation of photosynthesis does not show that it is a complex series of reactions with many intermediate stages.

$$6CO_2 + 6H_2O \xrightarrow[\text{Chlorophyll}]{\text{Light}} C_6H_{12}O_6 + 6O_2$$

Photosynthesis consists of two main stages.

1 The **light stage** involves the absorption of light energy:
  * some of which is used to split water, releasing oxygen;
  * some of which is used to form the energy carrier ATP.

2 The **light-independent stage** uses hydrogen ions from the light stage to reduce absorbed carbon dioxide and, with ATP, to synthesize organic compounds.

3 Bringing the two stages together gives:

$$6CO_2 + 12H_2O \xrightarrow[\text{Chlorophyll}]{\text{Light}} C_6H_{12}O_6 + 6O_2 + 6H_2O$$

The $12H_2O$ are necessary to show that all the oxygen evolved comes from water and not carbon dioxide (the simple equation above does not show this).

Photosynthesis and respiration

Plants also carry out respiration in which glucose is oxidized to release energy, which is used in metabolism, and carbon dioxide and water are produced as end products.

$$C_6H_{12}O_6 + 6O_2 \longrightarrow 6CO_2 + 6H_2O$$

Plants use up oxygen and produce carbon dioxide in respiration – the opposite of photosynthesis.

1 In the **dark**, plants take up oxygen, release carbon dioxide.
2 In **light**, photosynthesis proceeds faster than respiration, so they take up carbon dioxide and release oxygen.
3 At a low light intensity the two proceed at an equal rate; there is no gaseous exchange with the atmosphere. This is the **compensation point**.

Photosynthesis and respiration compared

	Photosynthesis	*Respiration (aerobic)*
1	Synthetic process (**anabolic**)	Breakdown process (**catabolic**)
2	Reduction, oxygen released	Oxidation, oxygen used up
3	Carbon dioxide and water used up	Carbon dioxide and water produced
4	Organic compounds are made	Organic compounds used up
5	Light energy trapped	Energy released
6	Proceeds only in light	Proceeds at all times
7	Only in plants with chlorophyll	In all living things

Mineral salts in plant nutrition

These are necessary in metabolism and in the synthesis of complex organic compounds. They are taken up from the soil as ions by the root hairs of young roots, by diffusion, active uptake or in the transpiration stream. They are transported in the vascular tissue to the leaves and eventually to the chloroplastids.

Element	*Ion*	*Role in plant*	*Deficiency symptoms*
Potassium	K^+	Protein synthesis, cell division, membranes	Leaves with yellow edges and dead patches
Calcium	Ca^{2+}	Middle lamella	Growing tips die
Nitrogen	NO_3^-	Amino acids, chlorophyll	Older leaves chlorotic
Phosphorus	PO_4^{3-}	Enzymes, ATP, DNA, RNA	Growth stunted, weak roots
Magnesium	Mg^{2+}	Chlorophyll	Older leaves chlorotic
Sulphur	SO_4^{2-}	Proteins	Young leaves chlorotic
Iron	Fe^{2+}	Chlorophyll formation	Young leaves chlorotic

Experiment to demonstrate mineral ion requirements of plants

1 Equal-sized seedlings are put in tubes containing:
   - ★ culture solution with all essential mineral ions;
   - ★ series of solutions, each lacking one mineral ion;
   - ★ distilled water with no nutrients.

2 Keep tubes at same temperature.

3 Cover tubes so no light reaches culture solutions and bubble air through at intervals to give healthy root growth.

4 Observe growth.

Experiments to show conditions necessary for photosynthesis

The effect of various conditions on photosynthesis can be determined by measuring the production of starch and oxygen. To test for production of starch:

1 dip leaf in boiling water for 10 seconds to kill cells;

2 place in hot ethanol for 10 minutes to extract chlorophyll;

3 wash in warm water and spread flat on white tile;

4 cover with iodine solution – **blue-black** colour shows starch present.

To show that starch is produced in the course of an experiment you must start with a **destarched leaf**: keep the plant in the dark for 2–3 days; any starch in the leaves will be broken down into sugars and used in respiration or transported to other parts.

Experiment to show chlorophyll is necessary for photosynthesis

1 Destarch a variegated plant (one with yellow or white patches on the leaves where there is no chlorophyll).
2 Expose the leaves to bright light for a few hours.
3 Remove a leaf and trace the pattern of the yellow patches.
4 Test the leaf for starch, trace the pattern of blue-black colour and compare with the pattern of variegation.

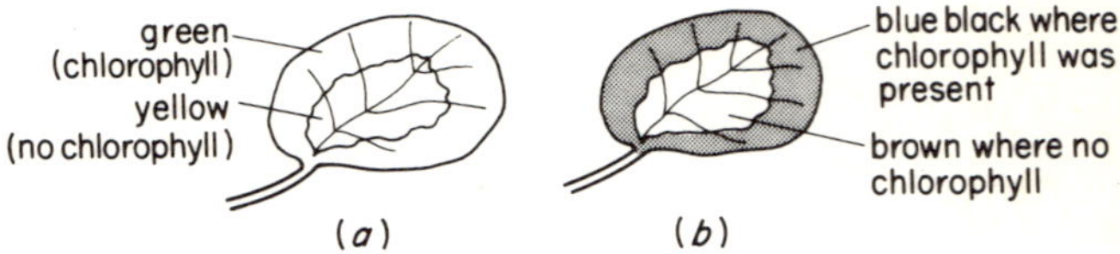

Fig. 3.4 *(a) Destarched variegated leaf. (b) Tested for starch after illumination*

Experiment to show that light is necessary for photosynthesis

1 Destarch plant and cover leaf with black paper stencil.
2 Expose the leaf to bright light for a few hours.
3 Test the leaf for starch and compare the blue-black pattern with that of the stencil.

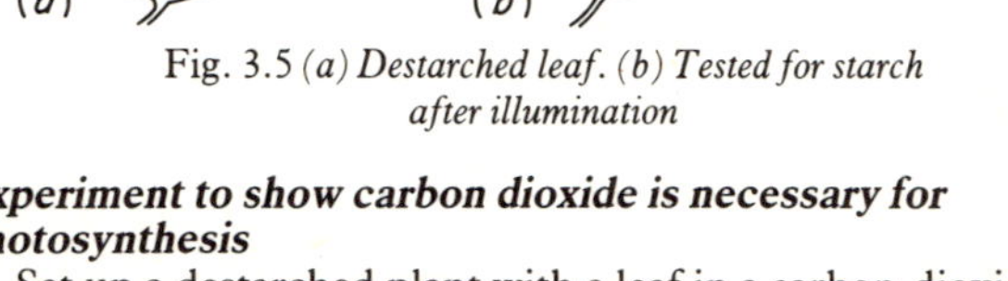

Fig. 3.5 *(a) Destarched leaf. (b) Tested for starch after illumination*

Experiment to show carbon dioxide is necessary for photosynthesis

1 Set up a destarched plant with a leaf in a carbon-dioxide free atmosphere as shown in Fig. 3.6.
2 Expose the plant to bright light for about 6 hours.
3 Test the leaves (the one in the carbon-dioxide free atmosphere and one exposed to normal air) for presence of starch.

4 No starch will be found in the leaf from the carbon-dioxide free air, but starch will be found in the other.

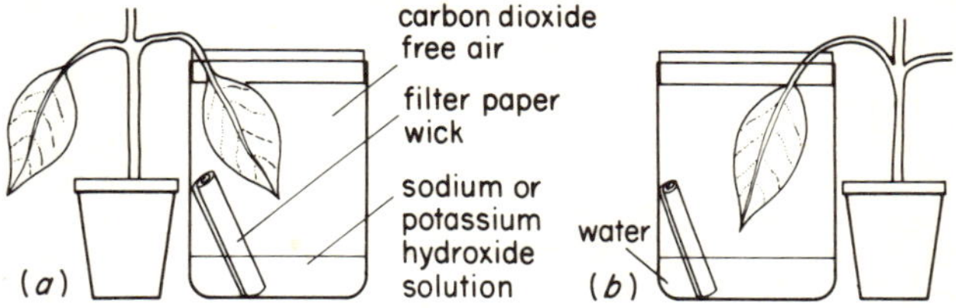

Fig. 3.6 *(a) To show carbon dioxide is necessary for photosynthesis. (b) Control*

Experiment to show oxygen is produced in photosynthesis

1 Select two similar samples of water weed.
2 Set up each sample in apparatus shown in Fig. 3.7.
3 Place one set of apparatus in the light.
4 Test the gas collected for oxygen with a glowing splint.
5 Other apparatus left in dark for same period as a **control**, showing oxygen not produced in dark.
6 Another apparatus without weed could be left in light to show that oxygen is not coming direct from the water.

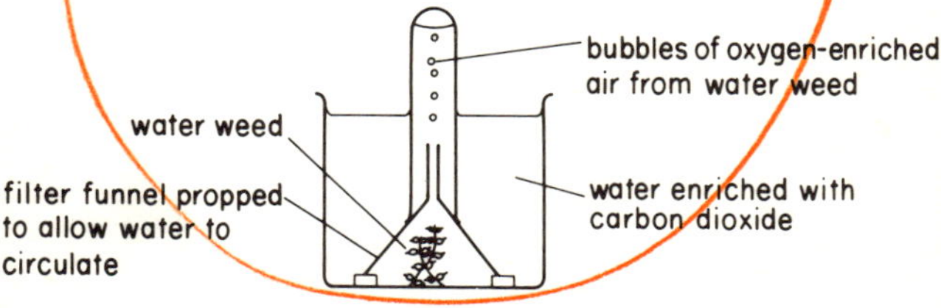

Fig. 3.7 *To show oxygen is produced in photosynthesis*

Holozoic nutrition in mammals

Animals cannot synthesize their organic compounds from simple inorganic substances as photosynthetic plants can; they have to have ready-made organic compounds in their food.

1 Mammals that eat only plants are known as **herbivores**.
2 Mammals that eat only other animals are **carnivores**.
3 Mammals that eat both plants and animals are **omnivores**.

Human nutrition

A balanced diet must contain correct proportions of carbohydrates, fats, proteins, vitamins, mineral salts and water.

Carbohydrates

1 Bread and potatoes contain much carbohydrate.
2 Carbohydrates provide us with most of our **energy**.
3 Carbohydrates include sugars and starch.
4 Cellulose makes up the bulk of plant material.
  * It forms the plant cell wall.
  * Digested in herbivores to obtain simple sugars.
  * It forms important part of our diet, providing indigestible bulk (roughage) which aids gut function.

5 All carbohydrates consist of sugar units.
  * A single unit is a **monosaccharide**, e.g. glucose.
  * **Disaccharides** consist of two monosaccharides combined, e.g. sucrose.
  * **Polysaccharides** consist of many monosaccharides, e.g. starch.

6 Some excess carbohydrates are stored in the liver and muscles as the polysaccharide **glycogen**.

Fats

1 Foods such as butter, cheese and eggs contain much fat.
2 Fats provide much **energy**.
3 Fats are made up of **glycerol** and **fatty acids**.
4 In addition to energy, some fats supply **essential fatty acids**, necessary for healthy growth and development.
5 Animal fats contain **fat soluble vitamins**, e.g. A, D, E, K.
6 Excess fats and carbohydrates are stored as subcutaneous fat. It acts as a heat insulation layer and for protection.

Proteins

1 Meat, cheese and soya beans contain much protein.

2 Proteins are needed for **growth** and **repair** of tissues, and supply some **energy**.
3 Proteins are composed of long chains of **amino acids**.
  ⋆ There are about 20 different amino acids which combine in different sequences and proportions to give all the different proteins.
  ⋆ Digestion breaks down proteins into their amino acids.
  ⋆ The amino acids are absorbed and resynthesized into proteins needed by the body.
4 The body needs 8–10 **essential amino acids**, from which it can produce rest of 20 amino acids.
  ⋆ Animal protein (**high biological value**) contains all these essential amino acids.
  ⋆ Plant protein (**low biological value**) does not always.
5 Excess amino acids cannot be stored by the body, so proteins must be a regular part of the diet.

Vitamins

1 Complex organic compounds needed in small amounts.
2 They are essential for health; without them **deficiency diseases** develop.
3 Vitamins are either:
  ⋆ **fat soluble**, e.g. A, D, E, K;
  ⋆ **water soluble**, e.g. B group, C.
4 Water soluble vitamins are easily lost in cooking and in excretions from the body.
5 Some vitamins are toxic in excess, e.g. A.

Vitamin	*Source*	*Function*	*Deficiency*
A	Liver, milk, carrot	Visual purple	Night blindness
B_1	Meat, milk, cereals	Energy release	Beri-beri
B_2	Milk, greens	Energy release	Pellagra
B_{12}	Meat, liver, yeast	Formation of RBC	Anaemia
C	Citrus fruit, greens	Connective tissue	Scurvy
D	Fish, sun on skin	Bones and teeth	Rickets
E	Milk, wheatgerm	Complex	Sterility in rats
K	Greens, liver	Blood clotting	Slow clotting

Mineral salts

Mineral	*Source*	*Function*
Calcium	Dairy products	Formation of bones and teeth
Phosphorus as PO_4^{3-}	Cheese, yeast	Formation of bones and teeth ATP, DNA, RNA
Potassium	Potatoes, nuts	Important in all cells
Sodium	Salt	Important in body fluids
Iron	Liver, eggs	Haemoglobin formation
Iodine	Fish, table salt	Thyroxine formation
Fluoride	Tea, water	Teeth and bone formation

toothpaste

Water

1 Solvent for all chemical reactants in the cell.
2 Transport medium, transporting substances in solution.
3 Medium for the diffusion of substances in solution.
4 Chemical reactant, e.g. in hydrolysis in digestion.
5 Support medium, e.g. providing turgor in cells and tissues.
6 Cooling agent in evaporation, e.g. the evaporation of sweat.

Food tests

1 Carbohydrates.

- **Reducing sugars**, e.g. glucose, fructose, maltose, lactose. Boil with Benedict's solution giving a yellow/green/red precipitate.
- **Non-reducing sugars**, e.g. sucrose. Boil with Benedict's – negative. Boil gently with dilute acid; make alkaline with dilute alkali; boil with Benedict's solution giving yellow/green/red precipitate (involves conversion of non-reducing sugar to its constituent reducing monosaccharides by acid hydrolysis).
- **Polysaccharide**, e.g. starch. Test with iodine in potassium iodide solution, giving a blue-black colour.

2 Fats. Rub on to white paper, giving a translucent streak.

3 Oils. Shake up with aqueous solution of red Sudan III; allow to stand; a red oil layer settles on top of water.

4 Proteins. Biuret test and Millons test; both hazardous.

Summary of a daily balanced diet

1 **Protein** – about 1 g per kg body weight, balanced for essential amino acids, for growth, repair and some energy.
2 **Carbohydrates** and **fats** – to supply about 12,600 kJ (3,000 kcal or Cals) energy for average adult each day.
3 **Vitamins** – about 15 different types, in very small amounts (total of about 0.06 g).
4 **Minerals** – about 15 different types, in larger amounts than vitamins (in total about 0.5 g).

Energy requirements

1 **Energy requirements** vary with age, occupation and whether a person is male or female. The figures here are approximate (1 kcal = 4.2 kJ).

	kJ	*kcal*
Babies	1,900	450
Child (8 years)	8,400	2,000
Youth (16 years)	14,700	3,500
Woman	10,500	2,500
Pregnant woman	12,600	3,000
Man	12,600	3,000

2 **Energy values** of some substances.

1 g of	*kJ*	*kcal*
Fat	38	9
Protein	17	4
Glucose	16	3.75
Alcohol	29	7

3 Some **food energy values** (kJ/100 g).

- ⋆ Bread = 1,000
- ⋆ Potato = 340
- ⋆ Cheese = 1,700
- ⋆ Milk = 280
- ⋆ Eggs = 610
- ⋆ Beef = 950
- ⋆ Rice = 1,500
- ⋆ Margarine = 3,000
- ⋆ Cabbage = 80

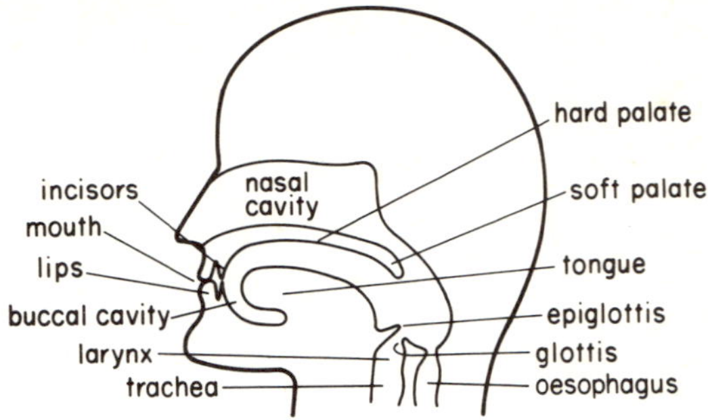

Fig. 3.8 *Air and food passages in head and neck*

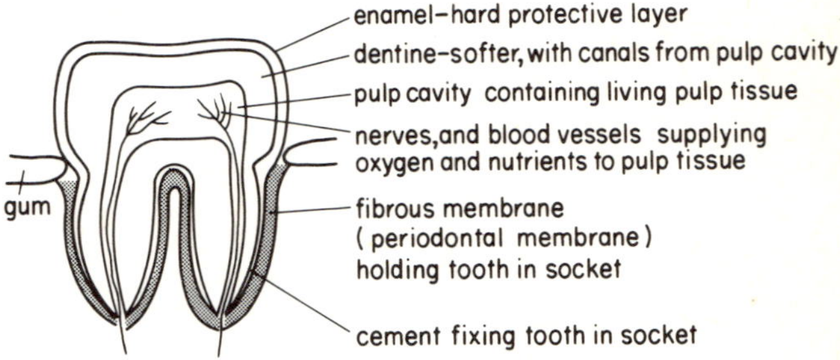

Fig. 3.9 *VS premolar tooth*

Dentition

There are four types of teeth in mammals.

1 **Incisors** at front, chisel edged for gripping, gnawing, cutting.
2 **Canines** – sharp, pointed for stabbing, tearing, gripping.
3 **Premolars** } at back, large, ridged with broad surface for
4 **Molars** } grinding and crushing.

The dental formula shows arrangement of teeth. In man it is:

$i\frac{2}{2}\ c\frac{1}{1}\ pm\frac{2}{2}\ m\frac{3}{3} = 16 \times 2 = 32$

1 i = incisors, c = canines, pm = premolars, m = molars.
2 Number above line = number of teeth in one half of top jaw.
3 Number below line = number of teeth in half of lower jaw.
4 Total = number of teeth in both halves of both jaws.

Dog's formula: $i\frac{3}{3}\ c\frac{1}{1}\ pm\frac{4}{4}\ m\frac{2}{3} = 42$

Sheep's formula: $i\frac{0}{3}\ c\frac{0}{1}\ pm\frac{3}{3}\ m\frac{3}{3} = 32$

Dentition in carnivores

Adapted for hunting and killing prey, eating meat, bone, etc. Teeth strong and sharp. Meat is highly nutritious and easy to digest, therefore needs little chewing.

1 Incisors – sharp, clamping action for gripping and tearing.
2 Canines – strong, sharp, stab and tear at prey.
3 Premolars and molars sharp – ridged '**carnassials**', scissor-like action due to jaw articulation with skull, only allows up and down action. Shearing action cuts muscle and bone.
4 **Jaws** have wide gape for biting prey, and strong muscles attached to strong skull bones for strong biting action.
5 **Gut** is relatively short and unspecialized when compared to herbivore gut as meat is highly nutritious and easy to digest.

Dentition in herbivores

Adapted for cropping and chewing vegetation. Vegetation is low in nutrients and difficult to digest due to the cellulose walls of plant cells; it is also abrasive due to the presence of silica in the cell walls, particularly in grasses. Therefore teeth adapted to chewing large volumes of abrasive material.

1 Incisors – strong for cropping vegetation.
2 Canines – reduced or absent, leaving a gap or **diastema**.
3 Premolars and molars – large, ridged, broad surfaces for grinding. Have persistent pulp cavities with good blood supply, allowing teeth to grow throughout life to offset wearing down of surfaces. Jaw articulation allows side-to-side grinding action as well as up-and-down movements.
4 **Jaws** have smaller gape than carnivores.
5 **Gut** is long and specialized for handling large volumes of poor food materials.

Mammals cannot produce cellulase enzymes to break down cellulose. Instead they have symbiotic bacteria in gut which secrete the enzymes. Herbivores have long intestines packed with these bacteria. The ruminants, e.g. sheep, cow, also have special anterior chambers of the gut containing more of the bacteria. They swallow their food into the **rumen** where it is partially digested into a **cud**, regurgitated, re-chewed and re-swallowed. The cellulose is digested.

Digestion in mammals

Some substances in the diet can be absorbed into the bloodstream without digestion, e.g. mineral ions and vitamins. Others have to be broken down into simpler molecules by digestion before they can be absorbed in solution.

1 **Ingestion** – the food is taken in.
2 **Digestion** – the food is broken down in two stages.
   - ★ **Mechanical breakdown** of the food into small particles by mastication and gut movements. This increases the surface area for action of the digestive enzymes.
   - ★ **Chemical breakdown** of the food into simpler molecules by process of hydrolysis – is catalyzed by enzymes.
3 **Absorption** – the food is absorbed into the bloodstream.
4 **Assimilation** – the absorbed food is used in the body (assimilation proceeds continuously, so is not a stage).
5 **Egestion** – unabsorbed food is eliminated as faeces.

Digestion in man

Buccal cavity

The teeth (and lower jaw), tongue, lips and cheeks chew or **masticate** the food and mix it with **saliva**, secreted by the salivary glands. Saliva contains water, mucus and the enzyme ptyalin, or **salivary amylase**, which catalyzes the hydrolysis of **starch** into **maltose**, a simpler disaccharide sugar. The saliva also moistens the food for swallowing, helps clean the teeth and mouth, and moistens the buccal cavity for speech.

The tongue and lining of the buccal cavity bear many taste buds.

When the food has been masticated it is formed into a **bolus** by action of the tongue, teeth and cheeks, and swallowed.

Oesophagus

This is a muscular tube leading to the stomach. The food **bolus** is passed down by reflex waves of contractions of the circular and longitudinal involuntary muscle of the oesophagus wall known as **peristalsis**. The entrance to the stomach is controlled by the circular cardiac sphincter muscle.

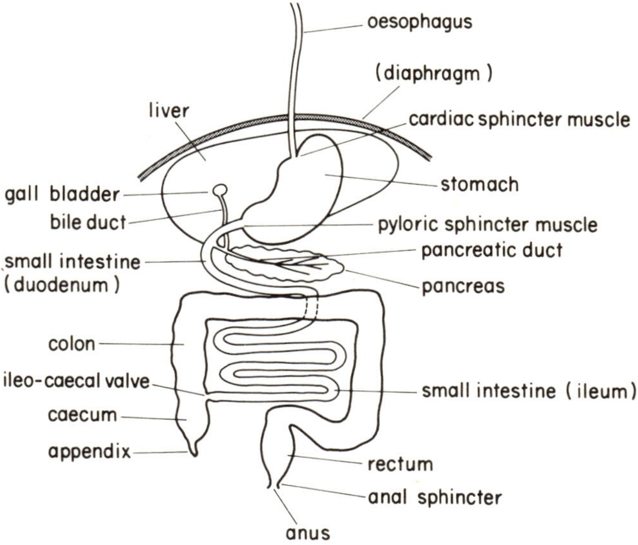

Fig. 3.10 *Alimentary canal, man*

Stomach

Food enters when cardiac sphincter muscle relaxes. The stomach is capable of stretching and acts as a temporary store for the food before it passes on to small intestine. Its wall has three layers of involuntary smooth muscle which contract in waves and mix the food with the **gastric juices**. The gastric juice is secreted by **gastric glands** and contains:

1 **pepsin** – to digest proteins to peptides;
2 **rennin** – to aid digestion of milk protein;
3 **lipase** – to digest fats to fatty acids and glycerol;
4 **hydrochloric acid (HCl)** – has pH of 1;
5 **mucus** – to protect lining of stomach from acid and enzymes.

There is a little absorption in the stomach, e.g. some glucose, alcohol, drugs such as aspirin. The food is pushed in small amounts into the small intestine by contractions of the stomach.

Small intestine

The first part of small intestine is the **duodenum**. It receives:
1 **bile** from the **liver**;
2 **pancreatic juice** from the **pancreas**.

Bile is formed in the liver and stored in the gall bladder.
1 It is an alkaline fluid, neutralizing the acid from the stomach.
2 It contains **bile salts** which emulsify (break into droplets) fats, increasing surface area for enzyme digestion.
3 It contains **bile pigments** – waste products from the breakdown of haemoglobin from old red blood corpuscles.

Pancreatic juice contains digestive enzymes in an alkaline fluid.
1 It neutralizes acid from the stomach.
2 It contains the following digestive enzymes.
   * **Lipase** – digests fats to fatty acids and glycerol.
   * **Amylase** – digests starch to maltose.
   * **Maltase** – digests maltose to glucose.
   * **Trypsin** – digests proteins to amino acids.
   * **Peptidase** – digests peptides to amino acids.

Intestinal juice is secreted by glands in the duodenum wall.
1 It neutralizes acid from the stomach.
2 It contains the following digestive enzymes.
   * **Lipase.**
   * **Amylase.**
   * **Maltase.**
   * **Lactase** – digests lactose to glucose.
   * **Sucrase** – digests sucrose to glucose and fructose.
   * **Peptidase (erepsin)** – digest peptides to amino acids.

Reflex peristalsis and shuttling contractions move food along. By the end of the small intestine digestion, and absorption of end products of digestion are completed. The **end products of digestion** are:

1 **monosaccharides** – glucose and fructose;
2 **amino acids**;
3 **fatty acids** and **glycerol**;
4 **vitamins, mineral ions** – need no digestion before absorption.

They are all soluble and capable of absorption.

Absorption of end-products of digestion is through wall of small intestine into capillaries of hepatic portal vein and lacteals of lymphatic system. Lining of small intestine is folded and covered with projections (**villi**), increasing surface area for absorption.

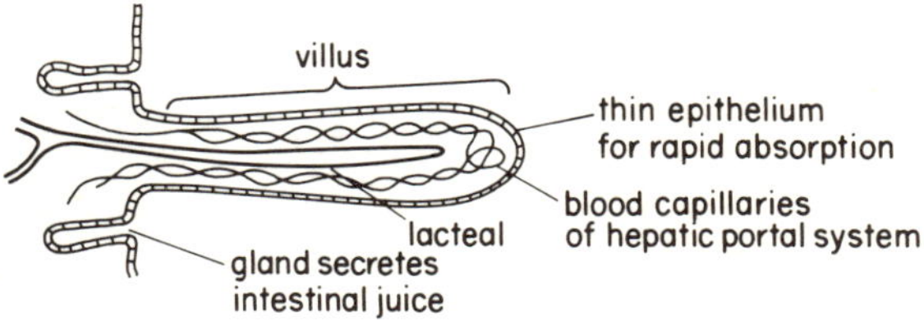

Fig. 3.11 *LS villus*

Uptake is either by **diffusion** or **active uptake**. Substances diffuse from regions of high concentration in the gut to low concentration in blood, down a concentration gradient. Active uptake needs energy from respiration and can result in substances being taken up **against** their diffusion gradient. Most fatty acids pass into the lacteals of the lymph system. Other substances pass in the hepatic portal vein to the liver for assimilation.

Large intestine

This consists of the:

1 **caecum** and **appendix** – contain symbiotic bacteria;
2 **colon** – main region for absorption of water, solidifying gut

contents to form faeces which pass to the rectum; contains symbiotic bacteria;

3 **rectum** – stores faeces before **egestion** via the **anus**.

Assimilation

1 **Glucose** – oxidized in cell respiration for energy; excess stored as glycogen in muscles and liver or as fat under skin.
2 **Fatty acids** – oxidized in cell respiration for energy; excess stored as fat under the skin. Fats important in cell membranes and fatty sheaths of nerve cells.
3 **Amino acids** – synthesized to proteins of cytoplasm, muscle fibres, enzymes, keratin, antibodies, etc. Excess cannot be stored and is deaminated in the liver, producing urea and residues that are converted to glucose and fat.
4 **Vitamins** and **mineral ions** – see pages 21 and 22.

The liver

The liver is the largest organ in the body. It has a double blood supply; the **hepatic artery** supplies it with oxygenated blood, and the **hepatic portal vein** brings blood containing absorbed nutrients from the wall of the small intestine. Functions:

1 adjustment of blood glucose concentration by interconversions to glycogen and fats and vice versa;
2 deamination of excess amino acids to produce waste urea;
2 storage of vitamins A, D and B_{12};
4 formation of bile;
5 breakdown of old red blood corpuscles;
6 storage of iron from haemoglobin;
7 formation of blood clot factors, fibrinogen and prothrombin;
8 detoxication of poisons, e.g. alcohol, drugs, etc.;
9 all these activities produce large amounts of heat. The liver is a major organ of **homeostasis**.

Enzymes

1 They speed up the rate of chemical reactions necessary for life, i.e. they are **catalysts**.
2 They are all proteins produced by living cells.

3 They are not used up in the reactions; therefore small amounts can catalyse large amounts of reactant.
4 They are specific, each type only catalysing a particular type of reaction.
5 Many need co-enzymes or co-factors to function.
6 They operate most efficiently under optimum conditions. Most have an optimum temperature range of 30–40°C and an optimum pH around 7.
7 At high temperatures and extremes of pH their complex structure is disrupted, removing their catalytic properties permanently. They are then said to be **denatured**.
8 Intracellular enzymes (those within the cell) catalyse all the chemical reactions of the cytoplasm and nucleus.
9 Extracellular enzymes catalyse chemical reactions outside the cell, e.g. digestive enzymes of gut.
10 They are often named after the substance they act upon, maltase on maltose, sucrase on sucrose.

Experiment to demonstrate enzyme activity

1 Obtain sample of saliva by rinsing mouth with distilled water.
2 Set up the following tubes and mix contents well:
   ⋆ A – 5 cm^3 1% starch solution + 1 cm^3 saliva solution;
   ⋆ B – 5 cm^3 1% starch solution + 1 cm^3 boiled and cooled saliva solution;
   ⋆ C – 5 cm^3 1% starch solution + 1 cm^3 distilled water.
3 Keep tubes at 37°C in water bath for a few minutes.
4 Take a sample from each tube and mix each with a drop of iodine solution on a white tile to test for starch:
   ⋆ blue-black colour = starch present;
   ⋆ no change in brown iodine colour = starch absent.
5 Repeat after several more minutes. When no further changes occur in the results with iodine solution, add some Benedict's solution to each tube and boil to test for reducing sugars:
   ⋆ orange-red precipitate = reducing sugars present;
   ⋆ no change in clear blue solution = reducing sugars absent.

6 **Results of test for starch:**
  - ⋆ A – starch absent;
  - ⋆ B – starch present;
  - ⋆ C – starch present.

7 **Results of test for reducing sugars:**
  - ⋆ A – reducing sugars present;
  - ⋆ B – reducing sugars absent;
  - ⋆ C – reducing sugars absent.

8 **Conclusions.**
  - ⋆ A – starch broken down into reducing sugars.
  - ⋆ B – boiling saliva prevents this conversion, showing there is an enzyme in saliva responsible for conversion in A (enzymes typically being denatured by boiling).
  - ⋆ C – starch does not break down spontaneously into reducing sugars (the absence of conversion in B might have been due to boiled saliva preventing spontaneous breakdown of starch), and there were no reducing sugars present originally in the starch (which might have been altered by boiled saliva in B).

Food chains, food webs and trophic levels

Photosynthetic plants make all their own organic substances from simple inorganic substances, using light energy. Some of these organic substances are used as energy sources in respiration and some are used as structural materials.

Animals (and fungi, heterotrophic bacteria and non-green parasitic flowering plants) cannot synthesize their own organic matter from simple inorganic substances using light energy, so require a supply of both organic and inorganic compounds. The organic compounds come from photosynthetic plants, either directly or indirectly via **food chains**, so all plants and animals are dependent on energy from the sun.

1 Photosynthetic plants are known as **producers**.

2 Animals are known as **consumers**.
  - ⋆ **Herbivores** are **primary consumers**.
  - ⋆ **Carnivores** are **secondary consumers**.

3 Fungi and bacteria living on dead organic matter are known

as **decomposers**. They are important in recycling materials.

4 Food chains interlink to form **food webs**.

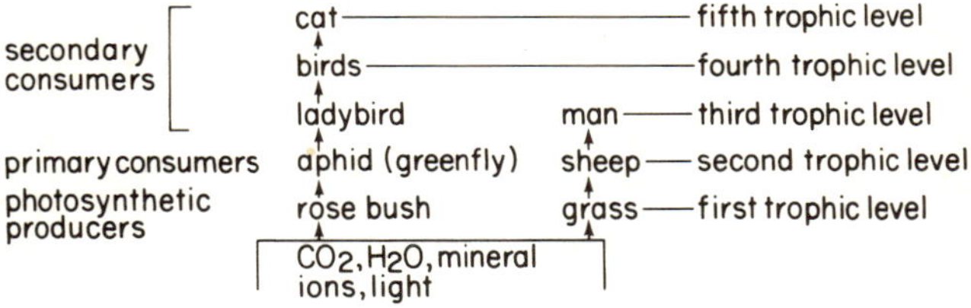

Fig. 3.12 *Garden food chain*

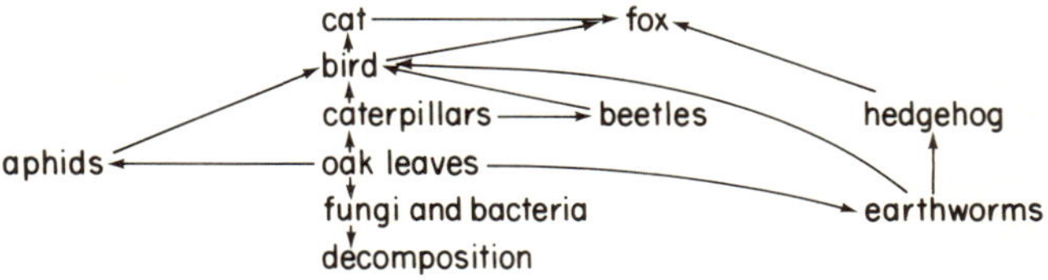

Fig. 3.13 *Food web*

Inefficiencies of conversion of material and energy from one trophic level to the next (only about 10% of the body material or **biomass** of one trophic level is converted into biomass of next trophic level) result in a **pyramid of biomass**, in which the biomass of each trophic level decreases up the food chain or web.

Cycles of materials

All energy that enters food chains and webs is eventually lost as heat, but materials are continually recycled.

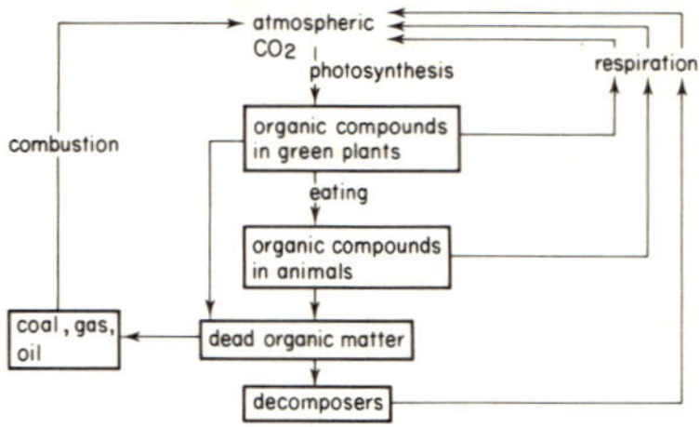

Fig. 3.14 *Carbon cycle*

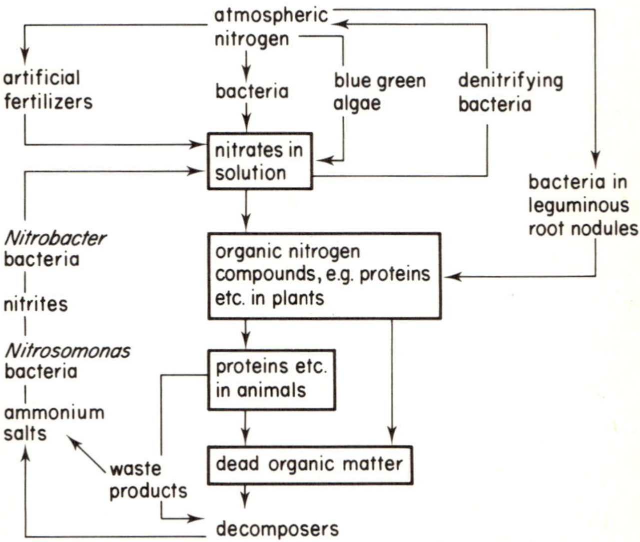

Fig. 3.15 *Nitrogen cycle*

All living things carry out respiration, resulting in **energy** from complex organic compounds being transferred to the energy carrier substance **ATP** (adenosine triphosphate), in which form it is available for the energy-requiring processes of life, e.g.:

1 synthetic chemical reactions building complex organic compounds from simpler ones, e.g. amino acids to proteins;
2 active transfer of substances across the cell membrane, e.g. the uptake of mineral ions by plant root hairs from the soil;
3 contraction of protein fibres, e.g. in cilia, flagella, muscles;
4 all energy is eventually lost as heat which speeds up enzyme-catalyzed reactions in the cell.

Respiration can be considered under two headings:

1 **cellular** or tissue or internal respiration;
2 **gas exchange** or external respiration.

Cellular or tissue or internal respiration

This is the biochemical process that occurs in the cytoplasm of all living cells, in which organic compounds, e.g. glucose, are oxidized to simpler inorganic compounds and energy is transferred to the energy carrier ATP. The process consists of a complex chain of enzyme-catalysed chemical reactions. It may be:

1 **aerobic respiration**, requiring oxygen:

$$\underset{\text{Glucose}}{C_6H_{12}O_6} + \underset{\text{Oxygen}}{6O_2} \longrightarrow \underset{\text{Carbon dioxide}}{6CO_2} + \underset{\text{Water}}{6H_2O} + \text{energy}$$

2 **anaerobic respiration**, not requiring oxygen in plants:

$$\underset{\text{Glucose}}{C_6H_{12}O_6} \longrightarrow \underset{\text{Carbon dioxide}}{2CO_2} + \underset{\text{Alcohol}}{2C_2H_5OH} + \text{energy}$$

ATP formation

Adenosine triphosphate (ATP) is formed from **adenosine diphosphate** (ADP) and **phosphate** (P) as a result of respiration. In releasing its energy it breaks down into ADP and P again.

$$ADP + P \underset{\text{Energy for metabolism}}{\overset{\text{Energy from respiration}}{\rightleftarrows}} ATP$$

Anaerobic respiration

1 Oxygen is *not* required. It is still an oxidation process as hydrogen is removed.

2 The respiratory substrate, e.g. glucose, is *not* completely broken down to carbon dioxide and water.

3 The products of incomplete breakdown, e.g. alcohol in plants, lactic acid in animals, are toxic and poison the cells if allowed to accumulate.

4 The incomplete breakdown of glucose releases less energy.

Some organisms are **obligate anaerobes**, i.e. they can only respire anaerobically, e.g. some bacteria. Others are **facultative anaerobes**, i.e. they can also respire aerobically in the presence of oxygen, e.g. yeast and our own tissues, especially muscle.

1 **Anaerobic respiration in yeast** (fermentation) is of great economic importance, e.g. in brewing. Yeast cells absorb sugars from the surrounding solution, carry out anaerobic respiration and excrete poisonous waste products (alcohol and carbon dioxide).

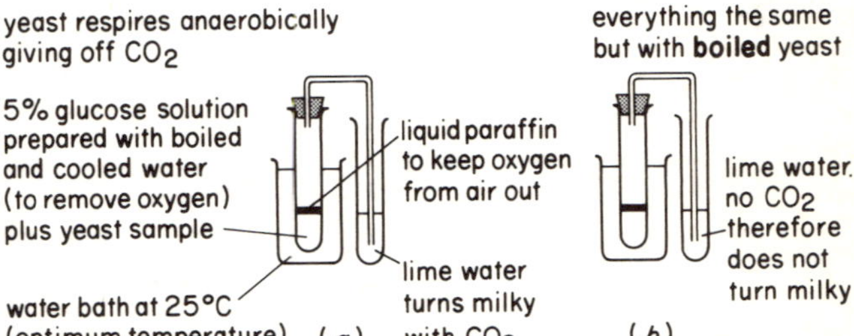

Fig. 4.1 *(a) To show fermentation in yeast. (b) Control*

2 **Anaerobic respiration in muscle** occurs if exercise is performed at a rate at which the blood cannot supply enough

oxygen to the muscle. This sustains the muscle's energy supply, but lactic acid accumulates and inhibits respiratory enzymes, leading to fatigue. As exercise eases, the body adjusts, more oxygen reaches the muscle and lactic acid is oxidized to carbon dioxide and water. Heavy breathing continues after violent exercise to pay off the **oxygen debt**.

Gas exchange or external respiration

Gas exchange between organisms and their environment is by **diffusion**, oxygen being taken up and carbon dioxide given off. Small simple animals have most of their cells in contact with or close to surrounding medium, and diffusion is sufficient to supply all cells with oxygen and remove carbon dioxide. In larger more complex animals, with a smaller surface area:volume ratio, there are usually:

1 specialized respiratory surfaces;
2 mechanisms for moving the external medium over them;
3 transport systems to pump blood past respiratory surfaces and transport oxygen and carbon dioxide to and from tissues.

This transport of gases to and from one side of the respiratory surfaces increases gas exchange by diffusion by maintaining steep concentration gradients across the surface.

Breathing in – inspiration

1 The **diaphragm** contracts and flattens **down**.
2 The intercostal muscles contract and move **ribs up** and **out**.
3 Volume of thorax (and therefore lungs) **increases**, and its internal **pressure** falls below atmospheric pressure.
4 Atmospheric pressure forces air into the lungs.

Breathing out – expiration

1 The **diaphragm** relaxes and moves **up**.
2 The **intercostal muscles** relax and **ribs** move **down** and **in**.
3 **Volume** of thorax (and therefore lungs) thus **decreases** and its internal **pressure increases** above atmospheric pressure.
4 As a result of this, air is forced out of the lungs.

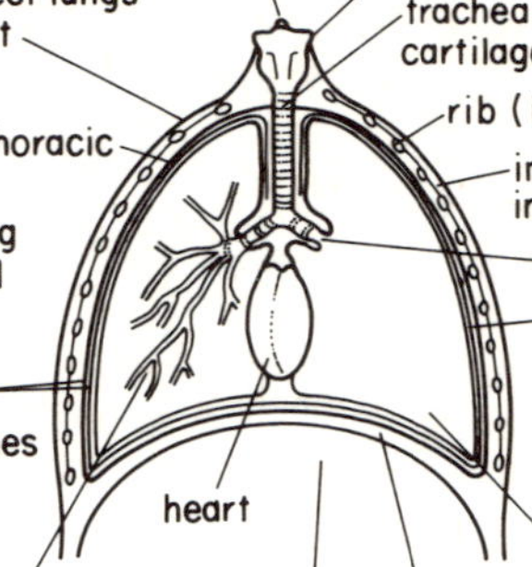

Fig. 4.2 *Thoracic cavity and contents, man*

Lung capacity

1 The **full lung capacity**, after the deepest breath, can be 5 l.
2 The maximum amount that can be breathed out is about 3 l, this being known as the **vital capacity**, i.e. the volume of air that can be moved over the lung surface.
3 The remaining air, that cannot be forced out, is the **residual volume**, this being the volume of the lungs when the thoracic capacity is at its minimum.
4 Normally only about 0.5 l is breathed in and out. This is the **tidal volume**.

Control of breathing rate

Voluntary control can be exerted over breathing, e.g. when

speaking. However, the basic rhythms are **involuntary**, being controlled by the rhythmic discharges of nerve impulses from the respiratory control centres in the medulla oblongata of the brain. These centres detect level of carbon dioxide in the blood.

1 If the level increases as a result of exercise, the nerve impulses to the diaphragm and the inter-costal muscles increase, resulting in an increase in breathing rate.
2 This lowers the blood carbon dioxide level.
3 The nerve impulses from the brain return to normal.

Gas exchange at the respiratory surface

Air warmed, moistened and partially filtered by mucous membrane and hairs of nasal cavity. In the trachea, mucus from mucus-secreting cells traps fine particles and ciliated epithelium sweeps dust-laden mucus up trachea, from where it is expelled by cough reflex. Eventually air reaches the **alveoli**, which are specialized for gas exchange.

1 They have a very **large total surface area**.
2 They have a **thin wall** – a single layer of epithelial cells.
3 They have **rich supply of blood** capillaries.
4 They have **moist surfaces** to absorb oxygen by diffusion.

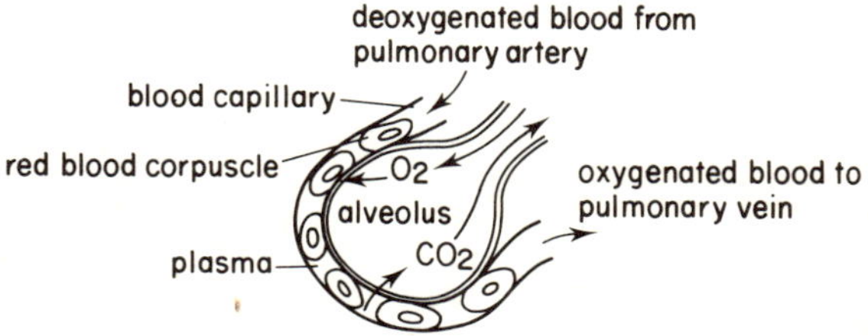

Fig. 4.3 *Gas exchange in lungs*

5 **Mucus** reduces loss of water by evaporation.

Inspired air is high in oxygen, low in carbon dioxide. Blood to alveoli is low in oxygen, high in carbon dioxide. Thus oxygen diffuses into and carbon dioxide out of blood, down their concentration gradients. As blood is continually moving past alveolar surface, steep concentration gradients for oxygen and carbon dioxide are maintained. Approximate composition of inspired and expired air:

	O_2	CO_2	H_2O	N_2
Inspired	21	0.04	1.25	78
Expired	15	4	6	75

Transport of respiratory gases in the blood

Oxygen diffuses in solution through walls of alveoli and capillaries into plasma and then into red blood corpuscles where it combines with **haemoglobin** to form **oxyhaemoglobin**. Carbon dioxide, carried mainly in plasma, diffuses out.

Experiments to demonstrate respiration

To show that carbon dioxide is produced by living organisms

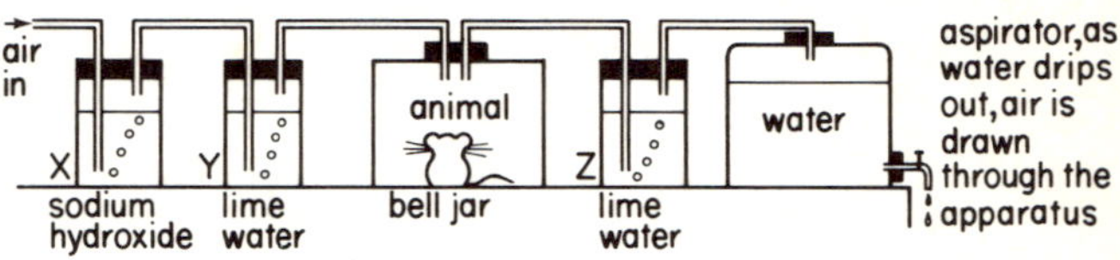

Fig. 4.4 *To show carbon dioxide is produced by living organisms*

1 In X the sodium hydroxide absorbs the carbon dioxide from air entering apparatus.
2 In Y the limewater remains clear, showing that carbon dioxide has been removed from incoming air.
3 In Z the limewater turns milky, indicating the production of carbon dioxide by the organism under test.
4 As a control the apparatus should be set up and run without a test organism to show that the change in limewater in Z is due to respiration of the test organism.

5 If a green potted plant is used as the test organism, the bell jar should be covered to exclude light and prevent photosynthesis and the soil should be covered as soil micro-organisms respire.

To show that oxygen is needed by living organisms

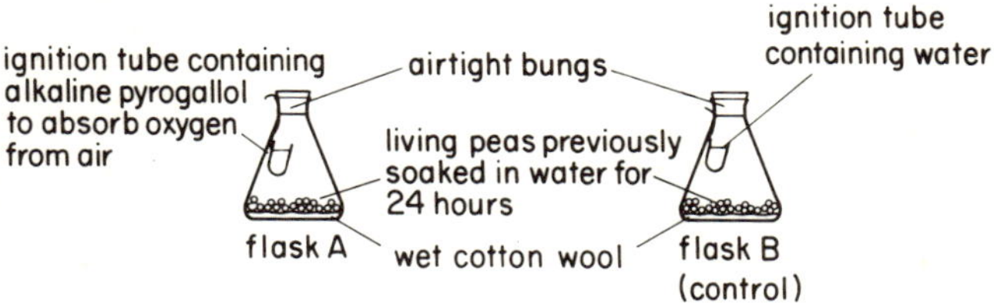

Fig. 4.5 *To show oxygen is needed by living organisms*

1 Set up flasks as shown, leave for a week and observe.
2 Peas in A germinate, peas in B do not.
3 This shows that oxygen is needed for germination – indirect evidence that it is needed for respiration.

To show that expired air contains more carbon dioxide than inspired air

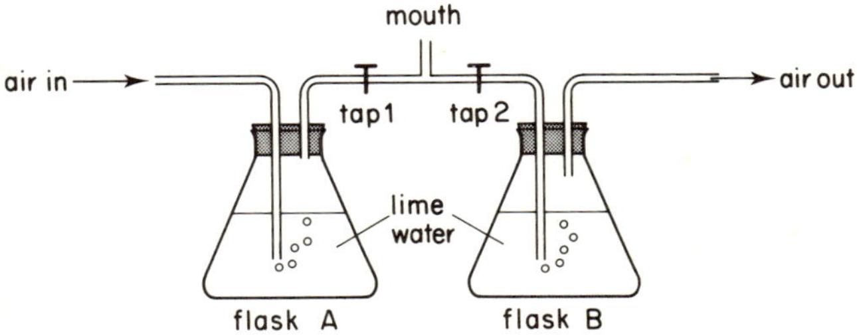

Fig. 4.6 *To show expired air contains more carbon dioxide than inspired air*

1 A shows the amount of carbon dioxide in inspired air.
2 B shows the amount of carbon dioxide in expired air.
3 Open tap 1, close tap 2 and breathe in through mouthpiece.
4 Close tap 1, open tap 2 and breathe out through mouthpiece.
5 The limewater in B will become milky due to the increased carbon dioxide in expired air.

To show that oxygen is taken up in respiration

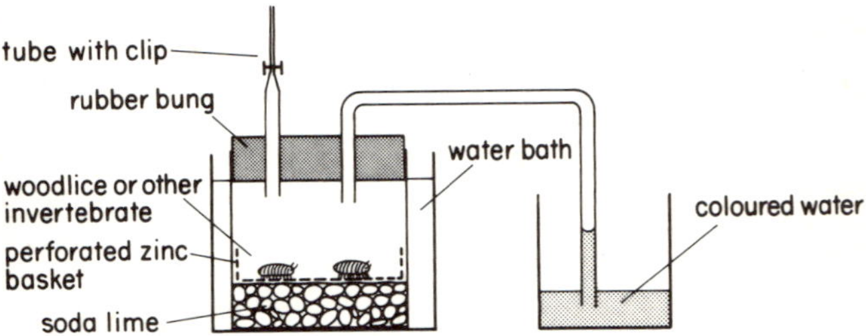

Fig. 4.7 *To show oxygen is taken up in respiration*

1 Soda lime absorbs carbon dioxide produced in respiration.
2 As the oxygen is taken up the volume and pressure of air in the tube decreases and atmospheric pressure pushes the coloured water up the glass tubing.
3 Distance the water moves in a given time is proportional to the rate of respiration.
4 The water bath prevents temperature changes which would alter the volume and pressure in the apparatus.

To show the production of carbon dioxide by use of indicator solutions

Indicator solutions change colour as pH changes, different indicators showing different colour changes, e.g. bicarbonate indicator goes from red to yellow with increasing acidity. Carbon dioxide dissolves in water to give an acid solution; as carbon dioxide is given off in respiration the solution becomes acid and indicator changes colour. The time it takes an indicator to change gives a measure of respiration rate.

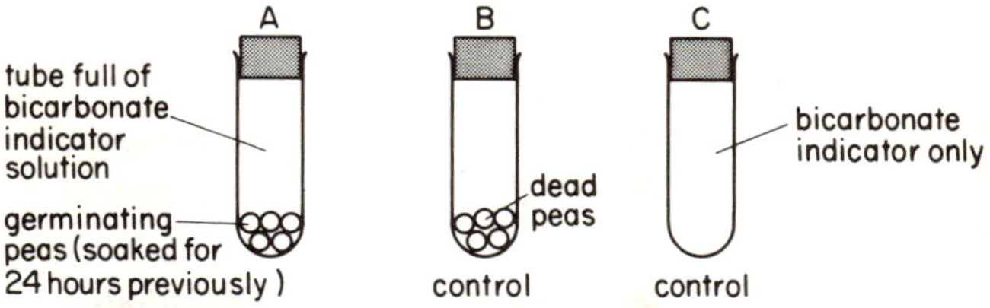

Fig. 4.8 *To show production of carbon dioxide in respiration*

1 A – the indicator changes from red to yellow as the peas give out carbon dioxide.
2 B – the indicator does not change.
3 C – the indicator does not change.

To show that energy is released during respiration

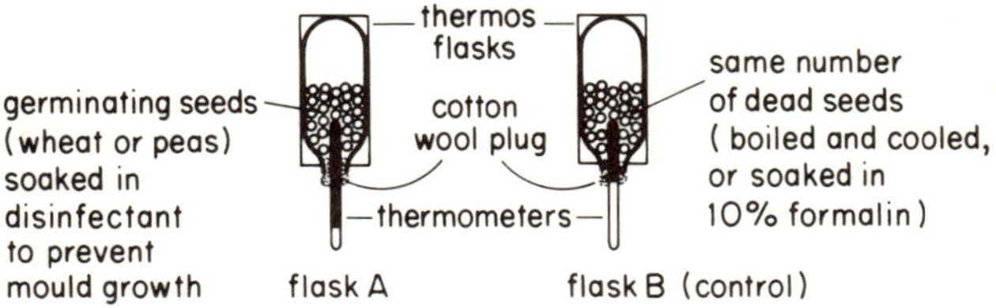

Fig. 4.9 *To show energy is released during respiration*

Flasks are set upside down as heat (energy) rises and there is less risk of heat loss through cotton wool. Also, carbon dioxide is heavier than air and so settles downwards and diffuses out through cotton wool, giving less chance of carbon dioxide inhibiting respiration.

1 Record temperature of flasks at start of experiment and at regular intervals over a period of days.
2 A shows an increase in temperature of several degrees.
3 B shows changes only if room temperature changes.

5 TRANSPORT AND CIRCULATION

In man, this involves:

1 the **blood vascular** or **circulatory system**; and
2 the **lymphatic system**.

The blood vascular or circulatory system

In this system a fluid – **blood** – is circulated through a system of blood vessels by the pumping action of the muscular heart.

Structure and composition of blood

Blood is a fluid tissue consisting of **blood cells** in a fluid **plasma**. The blood cells consist of the following.

1 **Red blood corpuscles** (erythrocytes) – 5,000,000/mm^3.
   - ★ Very small (7.0 μm) bi-concave discs with no nucleus.
   - ★ An elastic membrane allows them to squeeze through narrow capillaries.
   - ★ Formed in the red bone marrow.
   - ★ Contain iron-containing pigment **haemoglobin** which combines reversibly with oxygen to form **oxyhaemoglobin**. In this form oxygen is transported from lungs to tissues.
   - ★ They live for 3 months and are destroyed in the liver.

2 **White blood cells** (leucocytes) – about 10,000/mm^3.
   - ★ These are larger than red blood corpuscles.
   - ★ Two main types, **granulocytes** and **lymphocytes**.
   - ★ Granulocytes produced in red bone marrow, have granular cytoplasm, lobed nucleus and are **phagocytic** (engulf foreign particles) with pseudopodia.
   - ★ Lymphocytes produced in lymph glands, have large rounded nuclei and form **antibodies**.

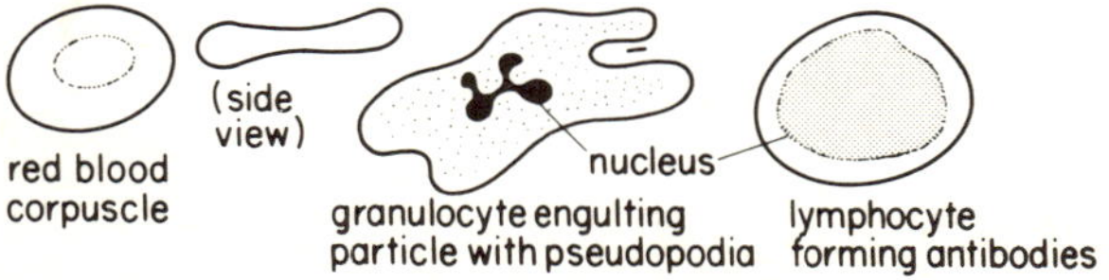

Fig. 5.1 *Blood cells*

3 **Blood platelets** – 400,000/mm^3.
- ★ They are fragments of cells (megakaryocytes) originally formed in the bone marrow.
- ★ They are important in blood clotting.

Plasma

A pale yellow solution in which blood cells are suspended. It has **constituents** which remain constant, and contains substances **transported** in solution from one part of the body to another, varying in concentration in different blood vessels, e.g. level of glucose will be high in hepatic portal vein after a meal and lower in hepatic vein, while level of urea will be high in renal artery and low in renal vein. Plasma contains the following.

1 **Water** – about 90% water and 10% materials in solution.
2 **Plasma proteins.**
- ★ **Fibrinogen** – forms fibrin fibres in blood clotting.
- ★ **Prothrombin** – forms an enzyme in blood clotting.
- ★ **Albumin** and **globulin** transport hormones, vitamins.
- ★ **Antibodies** and **anti-toxins**.

3 **Soluble end-products of digestion**.
- ★ **Glucose.**
- ★ **Amino acids.**
- ★ **Fatty acids** and **glycerol.**

4 **Mineral salts** as ions, e.g. Na^+ and Cl^-.
5 **Vitamins.**
6 **Hormones**, e.g. adrenaline, thyroxine, insulin, oestrogen.
7 **Waste products.**
- ★ **Urea.**
- ★ **Carbon dioxide**, in solution as bicarbonate ions HCO_3^-.

8 Some **oxygen** in solution.

Functions of the blood transport system

Transport of	*From*	*To*	*Method*
Oxygen	Lungs	All tissues	Oxyhaemoglobin in RBC
Carbon dioxide	All tissues	Lungs	HCO_3^- in plasma
End-products of digestion	Small intestine	Liver and all tissues	Solution in plasma

Transport of	*From*	*To*	*Method*
Hormones	Endocrine glands	All tissues	In plasma
Urea	Liver	Kidneys	Solution in plasma
Heat	Mainly liver and muscles	All tissues	In plasma

Defence against infection

1 **Blood clots** prevent loss of blood (usually externally but also internally) and entry of foreign material, particularly bacteria and viruses, at any break in the skin.

- ⋆ Damaged cells and platelets release an enzyme **thrombokinase**.
- ⋆ Thrombokinase (in presence of Ca^{2+} and vitamin K) converts **prothrombin** in plasma into enzyme **thrombin**.
- ⋆ Thrombin converts the soluble plasma protein **fibrinogen** into insoluble fibres of **fibrin**.
- ⋆ Fibrin fibres trap red blood corpuscles which dry to form a protective **scab**, under which new tissue is formed.

2 **Antibodies** are proteins which attack foreign substances known as **antigens**, e.g. the surfaces of bacteria and viruses act as antigens and stimulate production of antibodies.

3 In the same way antibodies attack the foreign protein of skin grafts and heart and kidney transplants, causing rejection unless antibody production is suppressed by drugs.

4 **Anti-toxins** are a special type of antibody that neutralize poisonous toxins produced by infectious organisms.

5 **Immunity** – once a person recovers from an infectious disease the blood still contains antibodies against it, and has the ability to produce more antibodies rapidly if the same infectious organism should enter the body again. This usually prevents a second attack of the disease, as the invading organisms are quickly destroyed by the rapidly-available antibodies – the person is **immune**. It is possible to develop life-long immunity to some diseases, but not to others.

6 **Artificial immunity** can be produced by **vaccination**, either:

- ⋆ introducing a dose of disease organism *not* strong enough to cause disease, but that *is* strong enough to stimulate production of antibodies, e.g. diluted sample or dead organisms; or

- ★ injecting antibodies formed by and taken from another host, e.g. horse (this type of immunity is short-lived as host's antibody-producing system is *not* stimulated).

7 **Phagocytosis** – some white blood cells engulf foreign particles with pseudopodia.

The pattern of major blood vessels in man's circulatory system

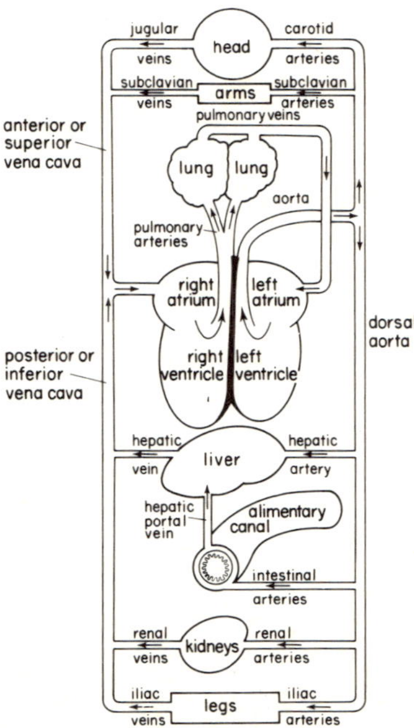

Fig. 5.2 *Major blood vessels, man*

1 This is known as a **double circulation**.
2 The blood passes through the heart **twice** during each complete circulation of the body.
3 The blood passes through the **right side of the heart** to the **lungs** in the **pulmonary circulation**.
4 The blood passes through the **left side of the heart** to the **body** in the **systemic circulation**.

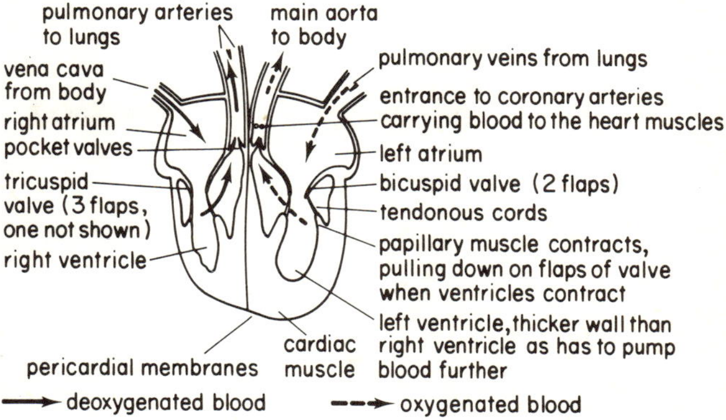

Fig. 5.3 *VS human heart*

The heart

The heart is a muscular pump situated in the thoracic cavity between the lungs. By its rhythmic contractions it pumps blood around the circulatory system. Mammals have a double circulation, with the blood passing through the heart twice in

each complete circulation of the body. There are **four muscular chambers**, the two on the right separated from the two on the left by a thick wall – the **septum**.
The start of the **cardiac cycle** is taken at the moment the ventricles have contracted to send blood to the lungs and the body.

1 The heart is empty and all valves are shut.
2 Blood enters both atria.
3 The bicuspid and tricuspid valves are pushed open and blood fills both ventricles, as well as both atria.
4 Both atria contract together (**atrial systole**) pushing more blood into the ventricles, which become stretched.
5 Both ventricles contract (**ventricular systole**) pushing blood up. The blood pushes the bicuspid and tricuspid valves shut, and the papillary muscles contract preventing the flaps of the valves opening up into the atria. Blood pushes semi-lunar or pocket valves open, and blood flows to the lungs and body.
6 The ventricles relax (**ventricular diastole**) and blood falls back into the pocket valves, closing them.

At this stage the heart is empty, all valves are closed, and the cycle is repeated. The cycle takes about 0.8 second. The heart sounds are made by the shutting of the valves.

Control of the heart rate
The average rate of heart beat in an adult is about 75 beats/minute, but variations from this are perfectly normal. Heart muscle (cardiac muscle) is myogenic, i.e. capable of rhythmic contractions without any nervous stimulation. However, the rate of contraction is controlled by nerves via the 'pacemaker' in the wall of the right atrium. Heart rate is also affected by hormones, e.g. adrenaline and thyroxine both increase the heart rate. The rate is increased by exercise, emotion (fear or excitement), via hormones, e.g. adrenaline, and the sympathetic nervous system.

Types of blood vessels
Blood vessels form a continuous system of tubes in which the

blood is circulated, each type of vessel being continuous with the next – it is a closed system.

1 **Arteries.**
   - ★ Carry blood away from the heart.
   - ★ Have thick muscular walls which contract to help pump the blood around the body – felt as the pulse.
   - ★ Branch to form smaller arterioles, also with muscular walls, which help to maintain the blood pressure by resisting the flow. Blood pressure is highest when the ventricles contract (systolic blood pressure) and lowest when they relax (diastolic).
   - ★ All arteries carry blood that is more oxygenated than that in the veins (except pulmonary and umbilical arteries).

2 **Capillaries.**
   - ★ The smallest vessels, forming a fine network in all tissues.
   - ★ They link arterioles to venules.
   - ★ Their wall is one cell thick, and permeable to plasma.
   - ★ Red blood corpuscles can only pass through in single file.

3 **Venules** link capillaries to veins.

4 **Veins.**
   - ★ Carry blood to the heart.
   - ★ Thin non-muscular walls contain blood at low pressure.
   - ★ Pocket valves at intervals prevent back-flow of blood.
   - ★ All veins carry deoxygenated blood (except pulmonary and umbilical veins).

Exchange of materials between the blood and the tissues

The pumping of the heart and the resistance to the flow of the blood in the arterioles results in the blood entering the capillaries under pressure. This results in plasma, minus some of its proteins, being pushed through the thin permeable walls of the capillaries. Nutrients, hormones, antibodies and oxygen in solution are thus carried to the tissues. Some of this **tissue fluid**, as it is now known, is drawn back into the capillaries, but the rest is drained away by the lymphatic system. In this way waste products, e.g. carbon dioxide in solution, are removed from the tissues.

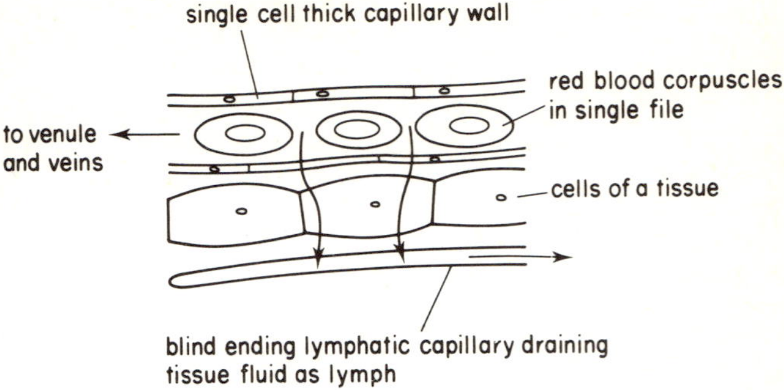

Figure 5.4. *Movement of tissue fluid.*

The lymphatic system

1 Lymphatic capillaries are blind-ending thin-walled vessels which drain tissue fluid away from tissues. They join up to form larger lymphatic vessels resembling veins (thin walled, with pocket valves at intervals).
2 The fluid (**lymph**) is pushed along the vessels by the squeezing action of the muscles of the body as we move; valves prevent lymph from being pushed in wrong direction.
3 At intervals are spongy swellings known as **lymph nodes** or glands. Lymphocytes and antibodies are made in these nodes, and lymph is cleared of any infecting agents before it re-enters the blood circulatory system.
4 The main lymphatic vessels join with the veins in the neck region.
5 The lymphatic system is one of the main defences of the body against infection.

Transport in higher plants

Terrestrial plants are rooted in the soil, from which they take up water and dissolved mineral salts as ions. Their leaves are held in the air to be exposed to sunlight and for the uptake of carbon dioxide, necessary for photosynthesis. Therefore substances must be transported up and down the plant to wherever needed. Generally water and mineral ions are transported up the stem to the leaves, and sugars are transported from the leaves to the roots (or food storage organs).

1 They are transported in long tubular **vascular tissues**.
2 Water and mineral ions are transported in a tissue known as **xylem**.
3 Sugars are transported in a tissue known as **phloem**.
4 These vascular tissues are found in **vascular bundles** in the roots and stems, and as **veins** in the leaves, reaching close to all cells.

Uptake of water

Water is taken up by the root hairs just behind the growing tip of each root. Root hairs are elongated single cells, and altogether have a very large surface area. Water is taken up by two means.

1 **Osmosis** – water moves from the dilute soil solution to the more concentrated solution of the root hair cell contents, across the large surface area of the semipermeable cell membrane. It continues to pass by osmosis across the cells of the root cortex until it reaches and enters the xylem in the root centre.
2 **Transpiration forces** – as water evaporates from the leaves, more water is pulled up the plant and into the roots.

Uptake of mineral salts

Mineral salts in solution as ions are also taken up by the root hairs. They are taken up by three means.

1 **Diffusion** from high concentration in soil to low concentration in root hair cells. They pass across the root cortex by diffusion until they enter the xylem tissue.
2 **Active uptake** – energy from respiration of the root hair cells is used to take up ions against their concentration gradient, i.e. from a lower concentration in the soil solution to a higher concentration in the root hair cells.
3 **Transpiration stream** – they can be swept along in the water being drawn in to the root by transpiration forces.

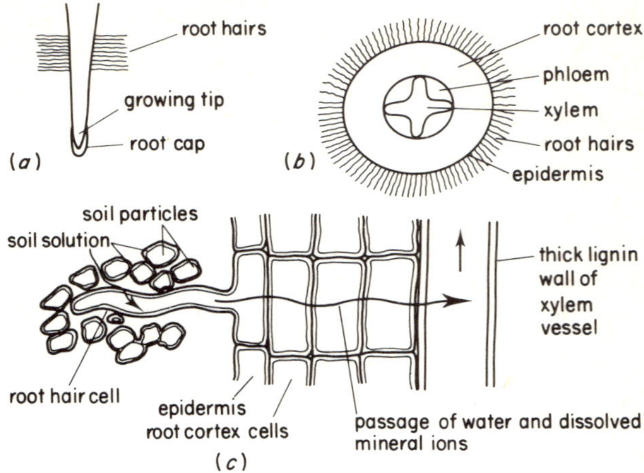

Figure 5.5. *(a) LS root tip. (b) TS root. (c) Water uptake.*

Transport of water and mineral salts up the plant

1 Water and mineral salts travel up the plant in xylem tissue.
2 Xylem consists of elongated, dead, hollow tubular cells with walls thickened with lignin.
3 They are arranged in columns, and their end walls break down so that they form long continuous tubes up the plant.

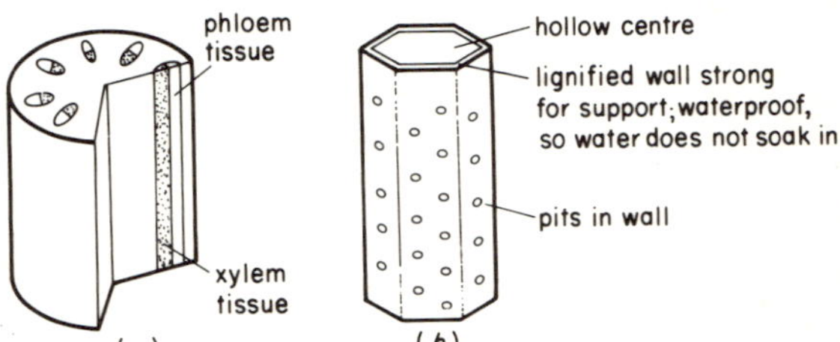

Fig. 5.6 *(a) Stem section showing xylem. (b) Xylem vessel*

Forces moving water up the plant

1 **Root pressure** – a positive pressure, developed in roots, pushing water up xylem vessels.
  * Depends on activities of living cells.
  * Shows seasonal fluctuations – greater in spring.
  * Osmosis thought to generate pressure.
  * Not strong enough to push water to leaves of tall plants.

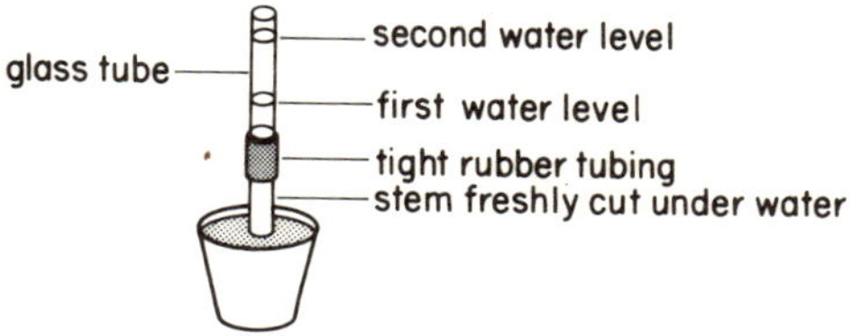

Fig. 5.7 *To demonstrate root pressure*

2 **Capillary rise** – xylem vessels acting as capillary tubes.
  * Their cross-section area is small enough for surface forces to raise water by capillary action.
  * Like root pressure, it is not sufficient to raise water to leaves of tall plants.

3 **Transpiration** – loss of water vapour from plant to the air, most of water being lost through stomata.
  * Water molecules attract each other and tend to stick together (**cohesion**). As water evaporates from leaves a continuous column of water (held together by cohesion) is pulled up xylem vessels in **transpiration stream**.
  * Air spaces in leaf are saturated with water vapour evaporated from mesophyll cells of leaf.
  * When stomata are open water vapour diffuses out to air,

which normally has a lower relative humidity.

* More water therefore evaporates from leaf mesophyll.
* Cell sap in these cells becomes more concentrated and water moves in by osmosis from adjacent cells.
* Water thus moves from xylem vessels in veins of leaf, across leaf cells to air spaces, and a column of water is drawn up xylem by cohesion.
* Column of water is supported by sticking or **adhesion forces** to side walls of xylem vessels.
* This process accounts for movement of water up trees.

Factors affecting the rate of transpiration

The rate of transpiration depends on the difference between the amount of water vapour (**humidity**) in the air spaces in the leaf and the outside air – the greater the difference, the greater the transpiration rate. Factors affecting the humidity:

1 **temperature** – warm air holds more water vapour than cooler air, so as temperature increases, transpiration increases;
2 **wind speed** – air moving past surface of leaf removes water vapour around stomata, increasing transpiration;
3 **rainfall** – the wetter the environment the more water vapour there is in the air at any given temperature.

Transpiration is fastest on dry, warm, windy days (not nights, when the stomata tend to be closed in most plants).

Functions of transpiration

1 **Transport** – of water and mineral ions from roots to leaves.
2 **Cooling** – evaporation of water has a cooling effect on the leaves, just as the evaporation of sweat cools humans.

Measurement of the rate of transpiration

Transpiration (loss of water from a plant) is difficult to measure directly. Instead the rate of water uptake by a plant is measured using a **potometer**, and is assumed to be equal to the rate of water loss. The potometer can be stood on a weighing balance and the loss in weight related to the water uptake.

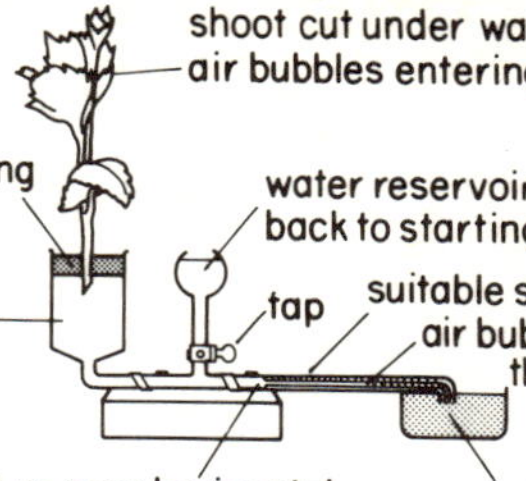

Fig. 5.8 *Potometer to measure rate of transpiration*

Transpiration under conditions of water shortage

1 **Dry soils** – when transpiration exceeds rate of water uptake by roots, cells lose water, lose turgidity, become flaccid and plant **wilts**. This lowers rate of transpiration by reducing surface area of leaf exposed to sun.

2 **Cold soils** – in winter, water in soil is not taken up by plant due to low temperature. To prevent transpiration deciduous plants lose leaves – impermeable **abscission** layer of cork forms across base of leaf stalk, leaf dies and drops off. Cork layer seals wound. In spring new leaf grows from axillary bud formed in axil of old leaf.

Xeromorphic plants have adaptations to reduce water loss by transpiration, e.g. reduced needle-like leaves, thick cuticle, stomata sunk in grooves/pits, and sometimes (cacti) swollen water storage tissues. Such plants grow in very dry conditions. **Evergreen trees** do not lose leaves in winter as they can withstand reduced water uptake by roots in cold soil.

Translocation

Transport of sugars (sucrose) produced by photosynthesis in leaves to wherever carbohydrates are needed, e.g. roots, seeds, fruits, storage organs. Sugars are transported in **sieve tubes** of **phloem** tissue – columns of living elongated sieve tube elements with perforated end walls (**sieve plates**). Mechanism of translocation not understood – cytoplasmic streaming plays part.

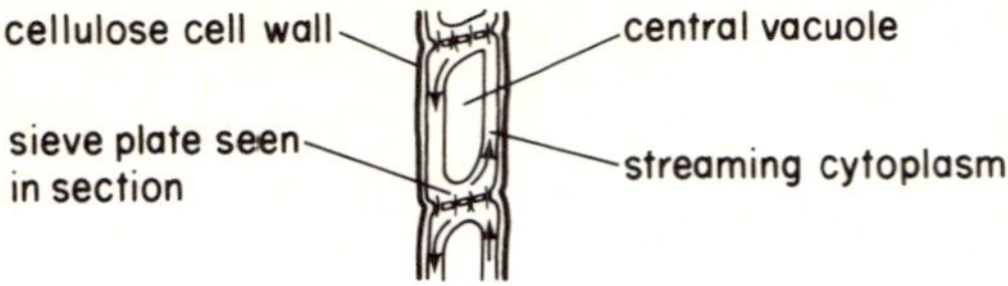

Fig. 5.9 *LS sieve tube, phloem*

Xylem	*Phloem*
Transports water and mineral salts	Transports sugars
Dead cells	Living cells
Thick lignin wall	No lignin
Few cross walls	Many sieve plates
Transport upwards only	Transport up and down

Excretion is the elimination of waste products produced by the body as a result of its metabolism, i.e. all the chemical processes necessary for life. In some cases the waste products are stored in the body in an insoluble (non-poisonous) form. Typically in animals they are removed from the body.

Excretion in mammals (man)

There are two main poisonous waste products produced.

1 **Carbon dioxide**, produced in respiration by all cells of body.
  - ★ Carried in solution in blood to lungs.
  - ★ Diffuses into alveoli of lungs and is breathed out.
  - ★ Most of the carbon dioxide is excreted by lungs.
  - ★ Carbon dioxide in solution produces acidic conditions; excess acid is eliminated in urine by kidneys.

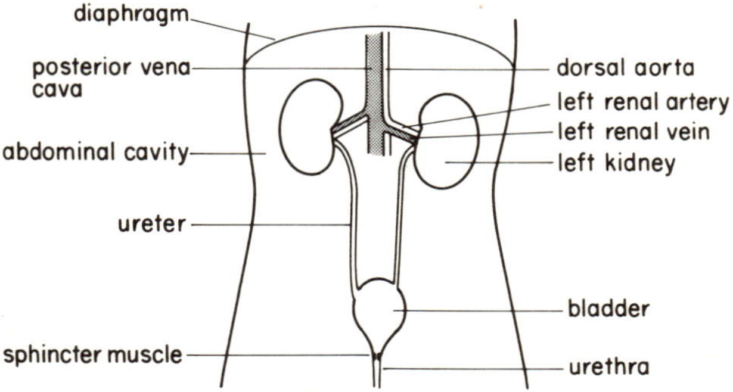

Fig. 6.1 *Urinary system, humans*

2 **Urea**, produced in liver from excess amino acids.
  - ★ Excess amino acids cannot be stored so are eliminated.
  - ★ Part of amino acid molecule is useful, but amino group (contains nitrogen) is poisonous and must be excreted.
  - ★ It is converted into urea, a soluble, poisonous waste product, in the liver.

★ Urea needs water for its removal from the body.
★ Traces of urea lost in the sweat.
★ Most urea is lost in the urine via kidneys.

The kidneys

1 Attached to dorsal wall of abdominal cavity.
2 **Renal arteries** carry blood to kidneys for:
   ★ removal of waste products, e.g. urea, excess acid;
   ★ adjustment of concentration.
3 **Renal veins** carry adjusted blood back into circulation.
4 Urine is carried in **ureters** from kidneys to the **bladder**, where it is stored before passing down **urethra** to exterior.
   ★ In male, the urethra passes down the penis, which also carries spermatozoa to exterior.
   ★ In female, urethra only carries urine, the reproductive tract (vagina) being completely separate.
5 Each kidney composed of thousands of tiny **kidney tubules**.
6 The kidney tubule (**uriniferous tubule** or **nephron**) is the functional unit of the kidney.
7 **Renal corpuscles** (**Malpighian corpuscles**) and **convoluted tubules** are found in the **cortex** of kidney.
8 **Loops of Henlé** and **collecting ducts** are found in **medulla** of kidney, giving it a striated appearance.

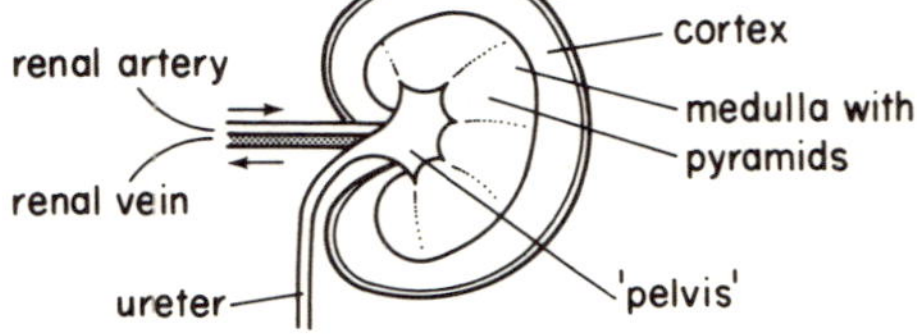

Fig. 6.2 *VS kidney*

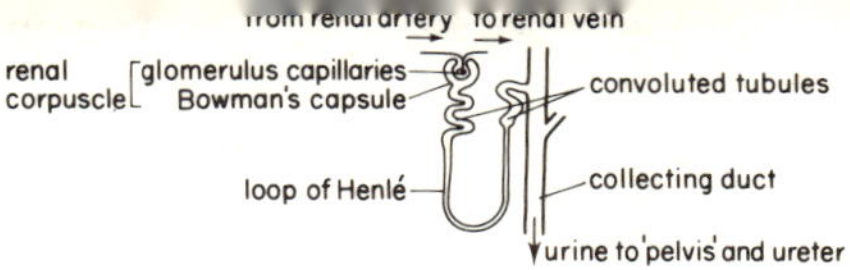

Fig. 6.3 *Kidney tubule*

Kidney function

1 **Filtration.** Blood entering kidneys is under pressure, forcing much of the plasma through the capillary walls, through walls of Bowman's capsules and into tubules.
- ⋆ Plasma is thus filtered through the various layers.
- ⋆ Larger molecules, e.g. plasma proteins, and red and white blood cells are retained in the blood.
- ⋆ This is known as filtration under pressure.
- ⋆ Filtrate contains water, salts, glucose, amino acids, etc., and poisonous nitrogenous waste product **urea**.

2 **Reabsorption.** In convoluted tubules most of the water, salts, glucose, amino acids and other useful substances are reabsorbed into blood. The remaining solution of poisonous wastes, e.g. urea, proceeds along tubule to collecting duct and ureter, as urine.

3 **Osmoregulation.** Kidneys also regulate concentration of body fluids in different conditions.
- ⋆ In **water shortage**, e.g. sweating, **anti-diuretic hormone** (**ADH**) is secreted by pituitary gland connected to brain. **ADH** travels in blood to kidneys, causing more water to be reabsorbed from filtrate into the blood. The urine volume decreases and its concentration increases.
- ⋆ If **too much water**, e.g. drinking too much, ADH secretion is lowered, less water is reabsorbed from filtrate, urine volume increases and its concentration decreases.

Excretion in flowering plants

1 **Carbon dioxide,** produced in respiration, is either:
- ⋆ used in photosynthesis in the light; or
- ⋆ excreted via stomata.

2 **Oxygen**, a useful byproduct of photosynthesis, is either:

* used in respiration; or
* excess diffuses out via stomata.

3 **Nitrogenous wastes.**

* Lost in dead leaves in deciduous plants.
* Stored in bark and heartwood of woody stems.
* Stored as crystals in living cells of herbaceous plants.

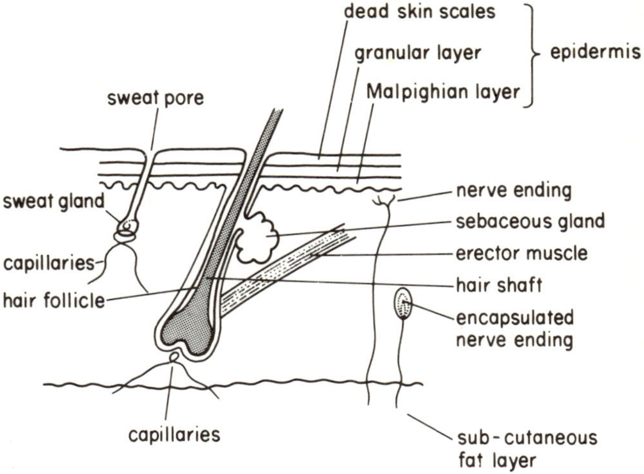

Fig. 7.1 *VS human skin*

Skin and protection

1 Dead, keratinized (horny) skin scales on surface of epidermis protects against mechanical damage (and waterproofs skin).
2 As this layer is worn away it is continually replaced from below by mitotic cell division of Malpighian layer.
3 The dead surface layer can become greatly thickened to form protective pads (calluses), e.g. on hands and feet.
4 Claws, hooves, horns, nails (develop from skin).
5 Melanin pigment in Malpighian layer protects against UV light in sun's rays.
6 Oil (sebum) from sebaceous glands lubricates passage of the growing hair through the follicle. It is also bacteriocidal (destroying some harmful bacteria) and waterproofs the skin.

Skin and regulation of body temperature

1 Mammals are **homoiothermic** (**endothermic**) – maintain a constant optimum body temperature.

2 To conserve heat, skin has:
- ★ **hairs** to trap heat-insulating layer of air (not man);
- ★ **layer of fat** to act as heat insulation.

3 **Regulation of body temperature when hot.**
- ★ Sweat glands secrete sweat onto surface of skin.
- ★ Sweat evaporates, absorbing latent heat of evaporation from body, therefore cooling body.
- ★ Blood vessels near surface of skin dilate (**vasodilation**) so more heat is lost by conduction, convection and radiation.

4 **Regulation of body temperature when cold.**
- ★ Sweat glands 'switched off'.
- ★ Blood vessels constrict (**vasoconstriction**).
- ★ Muscles contract (**shivering** – a reflex) to produce heat.
- ★ Hormones, e.g. thyroxine, stimulate metabolism.

5 If heat loss continues, the temperature control mechanism may fail to cope and body temperature may start to fall.
- ★ Temperature of limbs falls first.
- ★ Then temperature of trunk ('core' temperature) falls.
- ★ This is known as **hypothermia**.

Other functions of skin

1 **Sense organ** – variety of sensory cells in skin are stimulated, e.g. by heat, cold, touch, pain, etc. Some hairs have a specialized sensory function, e.g. cats' whiskers.

2 **Vitamin D synthesis** – vitamin D usually present in diet, but skin synthesizes it when exposed to UV light (in sunlight).

3 **Camouflage** and/or **display**, e.g. patterns of coloured hair break up outline of animal (zebras) or act as warnings (rabbits' white tail).

4 **Storage of excess fat** in subcutaneous layer of skin. This acts as long-term food store which gradually builds up if food intake is in excess of needs. Subcutaneous fat is unique to mammals.

The mammalian (human) skeleton

1 Acts as a **frame** for support of the body and its organs.
2 Provides **attachment** for muscles.
3 **Protects** organs and systems from damage, e.g. skull protects brain, vertebral column protects spinal cord.
4 Provides a system of **levers** for movement and locomotion.
5 Acts as **calcium store**, releasing calcium into the blood when needed. This is under hormone control.
6 Produces red and white **blood cells** in the bone marrow.

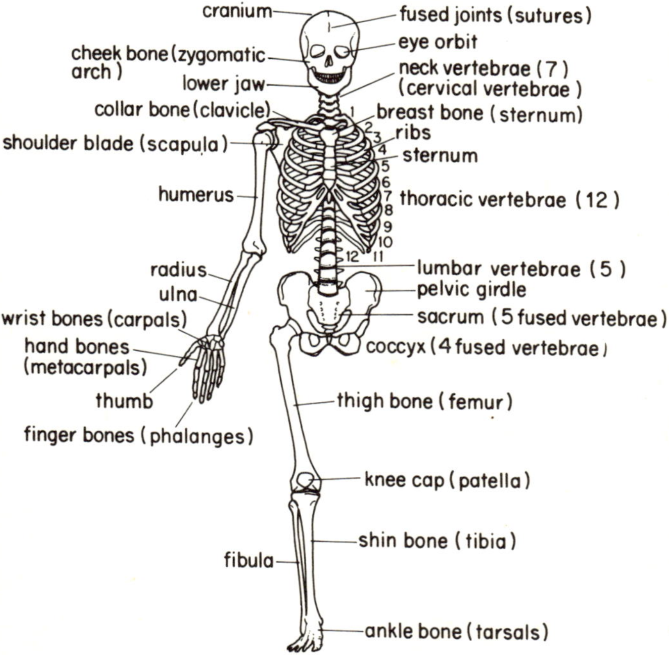

Fig. 8.1. *Human skeleton*

The skull

Consists of several bones fused by immovable joints (sutures). Cranium protects the brain; other bones of skull protect eyes, ears and nasal cavities. The bones also provide attachment for facial muscles and muscles that move head. Upper jaw is fused to cranium; lower jaw is articulated.

The vertebral column

Consists of several types of vertebrae.

1 **Cervical** or neck vertebrae (7).
   - ⋆ **Atlas** is the first neck vertebra. It articulates with skull to allow a nodding movement.
   - ⋆ **Axis** is second vertebrae. Allows atlas and skull to rotate from side to side.

2 **Thoracic** vertebrae (12) do not allow much movement in the thoracic region. They articulate with the ribs.

3 **Lumbar** vertebrae (5) – large, strong vertebrae with strong muscle attachment allow movement in lower back.

4 **Sacral** vertebrae (5 fused) form the **sacrum** which attaches the vertebral column to the pelvic girdle.

5 **Coccyx** vertebrae (4) – partly fused, greatly reduced in man.

Vertebrae protect spinal cord in spinal canal, allow attachment of muscles and limited amount of movement. They are cushioned by intervertebral discs of cartilage which act as shock absorbers. Paired spinal nerves emerge from between them.

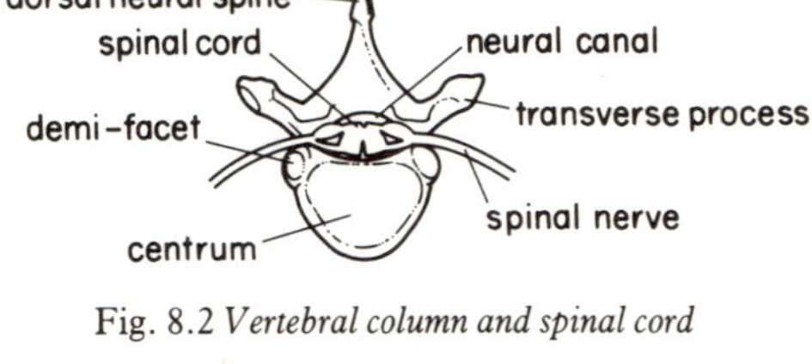

Fig. 8.2 *Vertebral column and spinal cord*

The ribs
Articulate at one end with thoracic vertebrae, and at other end by cartilage (allows movement) to **sternum** (breast bone). Last three pairs (floating ribs) are smaller and not attached to sternum. Ribs moved in breathing by intercostal muscles.

Pectoral girdle
Provides support and articulation for arms. Composed of:
1 two **scapulae** (shoulder blades) – broad flat bones embedded in muscle, not attached to vertebral column; muscles that move arm attached here;
2 two **clavicles** (collar bones) – rod-shaped bones, one end (along with part of scapula) forming socket of joint for head of humerus, other end fuses with sternum.

Pelvic girdle
Rigid ring of bone fused via sacrum to vertebral column. Provides socket of joint with head of femur. Protects lower abdomen and provides attachment for powerful muscles of legs and back. Cartilaginous joint at front (**pubic symphysis**) expands in female during birth. Female's girdle broader and shallower than male's.

The limbs
Based on pentadactyl plan found in all vertebrates with four limbs. Basic plan often modified, e.g. wing of bird, but all the limbs are **homologous** (of same evolutionary origin).
1 **Arm** – humerus, radius, ulna, carpals, metacarpals, phalanges.
2 **Leg** – femur, tibia, fibula, tarsals, metatarsals, phalanges.

Structure of bones
1 Bones contain living cells (**osteocytes**) that secrete bone.
2 Bone consists of fibrous protein (**collagen**) and calcium salts.
3 Bone is hard, tough and strong; capable of bending slightly.
4 It can be laid down in a solid mass (dense or compact bone) or in a honeycomb (spongy bone) for lightness.

Cartilage is a smooth tough material (gristle) forming smooth covering at ends of bones to allow free movement.

Fig. 8.3 *LS human femur*

Muscles

Muscle tissue consists of protein fibres capable of contraction. As each fibre contracts, becoming shorter and fatter, the entire muscle contracts and performs work. This requires energy from respiration (ATP); therefore muscle fibres have many mitochondria, and are well supplied with blood capillaries which bring oxygen and nutrients and which carry away toxic wastes.

1 **Cardiac** muscle – striated fibres, found only in heart wall.
2 **Smooth**, involuntary or unstriated muscle – found in walls of organs, e.g. gut, bladder, arteries. Slow sustained contractions controlled by hormones, e.g. adrenaline, and autonomic nervous system.
3 **Skeletal**, striated or voluntary muscle – bundles of striped muscle fibres which form muscles attached to the skeleton by **tendons** (strong non-elastic fibres). Contractions, under control of the will, result in movement and locomotion.

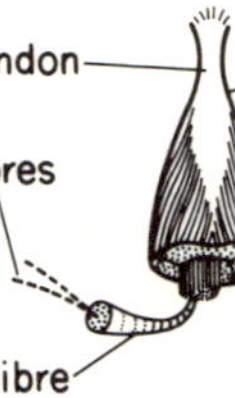

Fig. 8.4 *Skeletal muscle*

Muscles can only contract – they must be re-stretched by opposing muscle known as **antagonistic muscle**. Muscles usually occur in antagonistic pairs, e.g. muscles of upper arm.

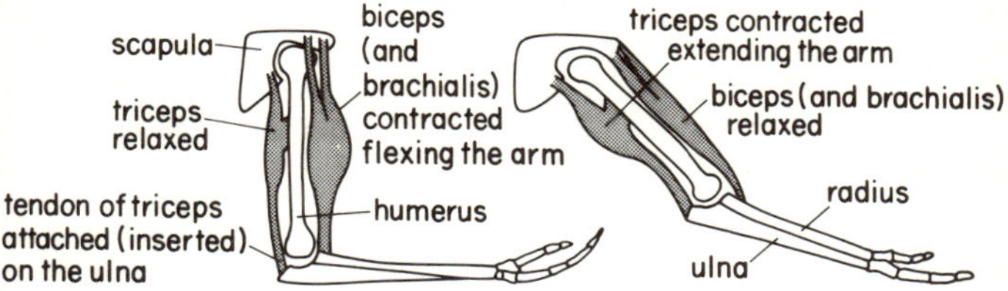

Fig. 8.5 *Action of biceps and triceps muscles*

Joints

Where two bones meet is a joint. There are three main types.

1 **Immovable** – bones are fused together and there is no movement, e.g. between bones of skull, in the sacrum.
2 **Slightly movable** – bones are separated by cartilage and bound tightly together by ligaments, allowing only slight movement, e.g. between vertebrae, between sacrum and pelvic girdle, pubic symphysis in pelvic girdle.
3 **Freely movable** or **synovial** joints – bones separated by cartilage and synovial fluid enclosed in synovial membrane which lubricates joint for ease of movement:

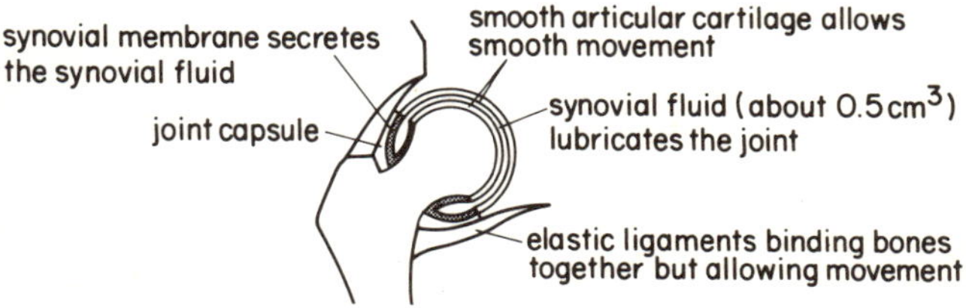

Fig. 8.6 *Synovial joint*

- ★ **hinge**, allowing movement in one plane only, e.g. elbow between humerus and radius and ulna, knee between femur and tibia;
- ★ **plane**, where two flat surfaces slide over each other, e.g. carpals of wrist, tarsals of ankle;
- ★ **ball and socket**, allowing movement in all directions, e.g. shoulder between humerus and scapula and clavicle, hip between femur and pelvis.

Bones as levers

A lever is a rod that moves about a point known as the **fulcrum**; it is moved by an **effort** that has to overcome a **load**. The bones of the skeleton act at a **mechanical disadvantage** (more effort has to be exerted than the load moved) but they act to increase the range of movement. Muscles can only contract a limited amount, but they are attached close to the joint and the end of the lever magnifies that movement many times.

Support in plants

1 **Turgidity** is important in all plant tissues with living cells, e.g. the non-lignified herbaceous parts such as leaves. In turgid cells the vacuole and cytoplasm push out against the slightly elastic cellulose cell wall, making the cell firm. Cells that lose their turgidity and become flaccid or soft as a result of shortage of water lose their supporting function, and the plant wilts.

2 **Thickened support tissues** with thick cell walls for strength.

- ★ **Xylem** – as well as transporting water, the lignified vessels and tracheids of xylem provide support, e.g. woody trees.
- ★ **Sclerenchyma** fibres are non-living lignified fibres important in support and protection.
- ★ **Collenchyma** have cellulose cell walls thickened in corners.
- ★ The thickened support tissues are distributed in a way that best resists the stress and strains the plant is exposed to, e.g. in the centre of roots, around the edge of stems.

Movement in plants

Apart from a few flagellate microscopic algae, plants cannot carry out locomotion (move from place to place).

Their active movement (as opposed to passive movement, e.g. being blown by the wind) typically involves **growth**. As a result it is usually slow and its effects can be permanent, e.g. if a stem moves by bending towards light, that part of the stem remains bent. Plant movement is restricted to specialized regions.

Automatic (autonomic) movements in plants

This type of movement occurs automatically, not in response to a stimulus. An example is seen in the circular movements of the stem tips of climbing plants which help the plants to locate a support around which they grow.

Stimulus movements in plants

These movements occur in response to a stimulus.

1 Non-directional (**nastic**) movements do not occur in any particular direction, e.g.:
   - ⋆ crocus and tulip flowers close at night in response to a drop in temperature ('sleep movements');
   - ⋆ dandelions and daisies close in response to decreasing light at dusk;
   - ⋆ leaves of clover and runner beans fold up at night;
   - ⋆ spiked leaves of Venus fly trap close around an insect.

2 **Tactic** movements.
   - ⋆ These movements are seen in single cells that move towards a favourable stimulus (positive taxis), or away from an unfavourable stimulus (negative taxis).
   - ⋆ For example, the positive phototaxis of *Euglena* swimming towards light so that it can photosynthesize.

3 Directional growth movements (**tropisms**).
   - ⋆ These movements involve a part of a plant growing towards or away from a stimulus.
   - ⋆ This bending occurs as a result of the cells on one side of the stem or root growing by extension more than the cells on the other side.
   - ⋆ This increased growth, on one side of a stem for example, is caused by an increased level of the plant growth hormone **auxin** on that side.

- ★ Auxin is made in the stem and root tips and is passed back to the zone of elongation, where it stimulates cell extension.
- ★ The reason for the unequal distribution of auxin in tropisms is unknown.
- ★ The response to unequal illumination is **phototropism**. Shoots and leaves are positively phototropic, growing towards light, which is necessary for photosynthesis.
- ★ The response to gravity is **geotropism**. Roots are positively geotropic, growing down towards gravity. Shoots are negatively geotropic, growing away from gravity.
- ★ The response to chemicals is **chemotropism**. Pollen tubes are positively chemotropic towards the ovule.

Experiments to demonstrate tropisms

1 Positive phototropism in shoots.

- ★ One seedling exposed to light from one side only.
- ★ Another seedling placed under similar conditions, but rotated on slowly revolving turntable (**clinostat**), so that plant is exposed to light on all sides.

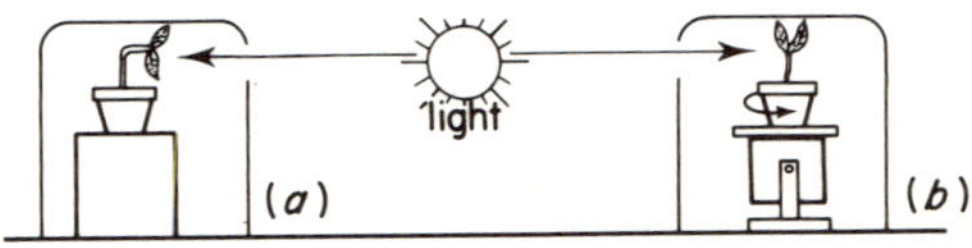

Fig. 8.7 *(a) To show positive phototropism in shoots. (b) Control*

2 That the shoot tip is the sensitive region detecting the stimulus.

- ★ One set of seedlings exposed to light from one side only.
- ★ Another set is de-topped (tips of shoot cut off) and exposed to light from one side only.

Fig. 8.8 *(a) To show shoot tip is light-sensitive. (b) Control*

3 Negative geotropism in shoots and positive geotropism in roots.

- ★ A seedling is held in a horizontal position so that one side of the shoot or root is exposed to gravity.
- ★ Another is set horizontally on a slowly revolving clinostat so that all sides are exposed to gravity in continuous sequence.

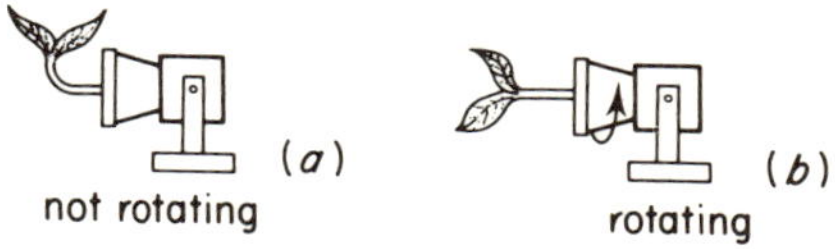

Fig. 8.9 *(a) To show negative geotropism in shoots. (b) Control*

Fig. 8.10 *(a) To show positive geotropism in roots. (b) Control*

9 NERVOUS CONTROL AND COORDINATION

Mammalian nervous system

1 **Central nervous system** (CNS).
  - ⋆ Brain.
  - ⋆ Spinal cord.

2 The central nervous system receives, relays, coordinates, interprets, and transmits nervous impulses.

3 **Peripheral nervous system.**
  - ⋆ Cranial nerves.
  - ⋆ Spinal nerves.

4 The peripheral nervous system consists of:
  - ⋆ **sensory** (afferent) nerves carrying impulses to CNS from sense organs;
  - ⋆ **motor** (efferent) nerves carry impulses from CNS to effector regions where actions occur, e.g. muscles, glands.

Nerve cells

Functional unit of nervous system is nerve cell or neurone, Complexity of nervous system is due to millions of these cells and their complex interconnections. Three main types of nerve cells.

1 **Sensory** neurones.
2 **Motor** neurones.
3 **Intermediate** neurones.
4 Neuroglial cells support and supply nutrients to neurones.
5 Nerves consist of bundles of the long processes of neurones.

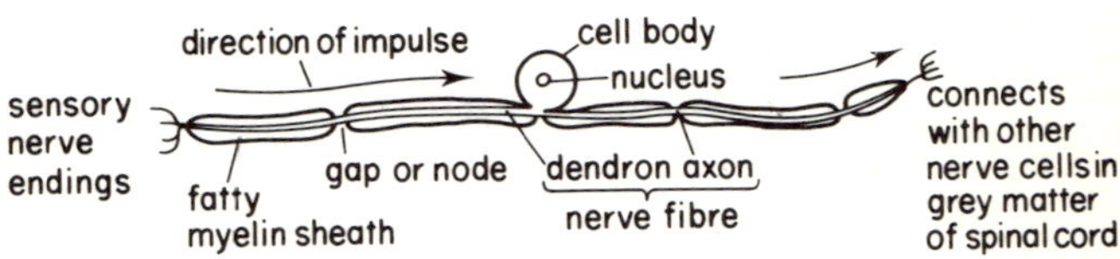

Fig. 9.1 *Sensory neurone*

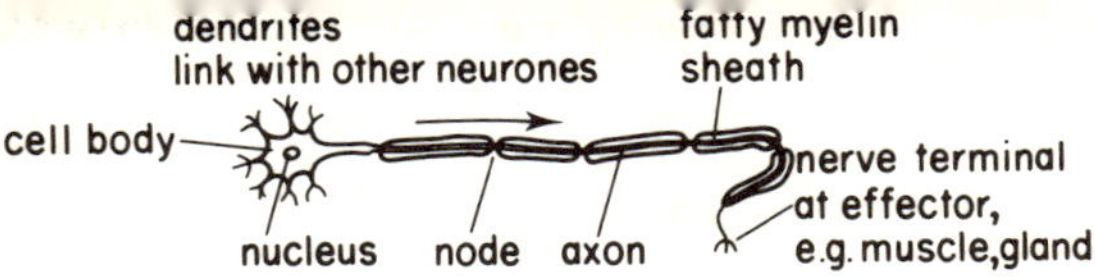

Fig. 9.2 *Motor neurone*

Reflex action

Simplest action of nervous system is a **reflex action** – (automatic response to stimulus, e.g. pain) based on **reflex arc** (series of two or more neurones). Simplest reflex arcs are based on spinal cord.

1 A stimulus is detected by sensory receptor cells in skin.
2 Sensory neurones transmit impulses from receptors to the intermediate or relay neurones in the CNS.
3 Intermediate neurones transmit impulses to motor neurones.
4 Motor neurones transmit impulses to effector, e.g. muscle.
5 The muscle contracts in response to the stimulus.
6 At the same time impulses are transmitted to the brain for information, so that the stimulus is perceived.

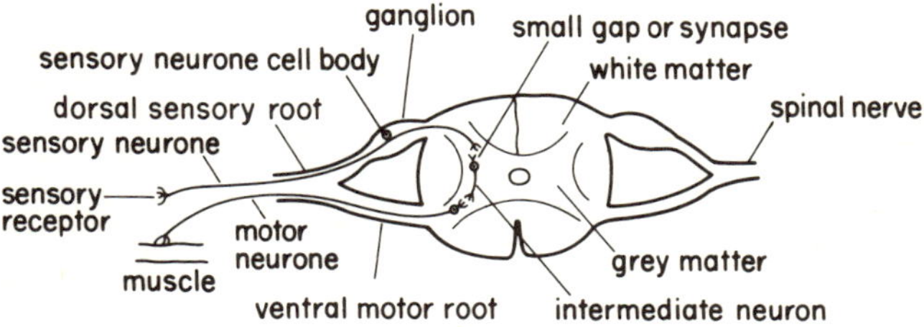

Fig. 9.3 *TS spinal cord and simple reflex arc*

The spinal cord

The spinal cord runs from the brain down the **neural canal** in the vertebral column. It is also protected by membranes (**meninges**). It gives rise to paired spinal nerves along its length.

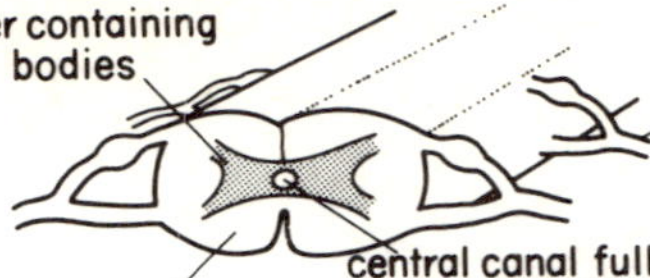

Fig. 9.4 *Spinal cord and spinal nerves*

The brain

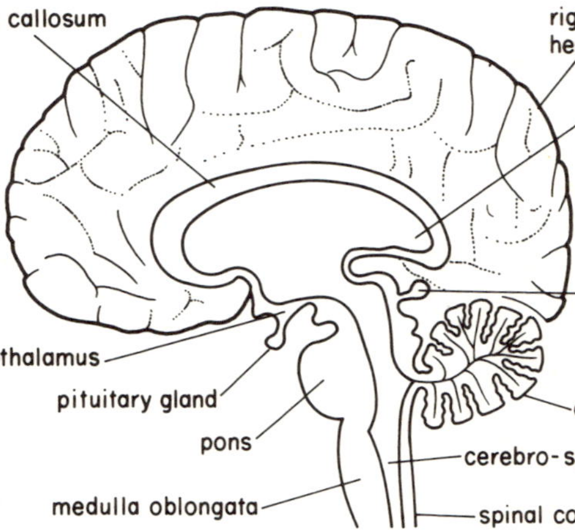

Fig. 9.5 *VS human brain*

The brain receives sensory impulses from all over the body; it is particularly associated with the major sense organs – eyes and ears. These impulses are interpreted and motor impulses transmitted along motor neurones to all parts of the body. The complexity of the connections between the neurones results in the brain having 'higher functions' that are not understood yet:

1 **instinct** – genetically determined, fixed actions, typical of all members of a species, not dependent on learning, e.g. many courtship displays, early feeding of the young, etc.;
2 **memory**, **learning** – memory of past stimuli used to decide correct response to particular situation, i.e. behaviour is modified in light of past experience, e.g. **conditioned reflex** where response to a particular stimulus is 'conditioned' to occur in response to a different stimulus:
   - ⋆ hungry dog sees (and smells) food, produces saliva;
   - ⋆ dog shown food, bell rung – produces saliva;
   - ⋆ many repetitions of this;
   - ⋆ dog *not* shown food but bell rung – produces saliva;
   - ⋆ original response (saliva production) has been conditioned to occur with a new stimulus (bell).

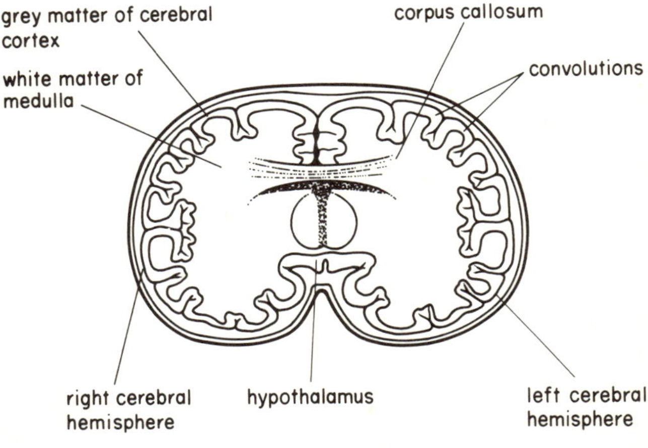

Fig. 9.6 *Cross-section human brain*

Regions of the brain

1 **Cerebral hemispheres** – the cerebrum is enlarged into two cerebral hemispheres. The surface of the cerebral hemispheres is folded (convoluted), increasing the amount of grey matter of cerebral cortex – region of millions of nerve cell bodies and their interconnections (synapses), and centre of higher functions of brain, e.g. memory, thought, intelligence, emotions, sight, hearing, etc. Right cerebral hemisphere controls left side of the body; left cerebral hemisphere controls right side of body. The two hemispheres are linked and coordinated by a broad band of nerve fibres. (**corpus callosum**).
2 **Hypothalamus** – centre of complex reflexes controlling homeostasis of body, e.g. temperature control, osmoregulation, etc. Also closely connected with **pituitary gland** (control centre of hormone secreting system).
3 **Cerebellum** – control centre of the major reflexes involved in balance and movement.
4 **Medulla oblongata** – centre of major reflexes, e.g. breathing, heart rate, swallowing, blinking, etc.

Mammalian sensory receptors

Sensory receptors detect changes in conditions (**stimuli**). They are usually specialized in their sensitivity to particular stimuli. When stimulated they initiate a stream of impulses in sensory neurones linking them with CNS, where the sensation of the stimulus is felt. Different types of sensory receptor cells are for:

1 **touch** and **pressure** – in the skin;
2 **pain** – in the skin, and in other organs;
3 **temperature** – in the skin;
4 **stretch** – in the muscles and tendons;
5 **smell** (olfactory) – lining the nasal cavity;
6 **taste** – in the taste buds on the tongue, and lining the mouth;
7 **light** – in the retina of the eye;
8 **sound** – in the inner ear;
9 **movement** – in the inner ear;
10 **gravity** – in the inner ear.

The eye

Light rays reflected from an object are focused to form an image on the light sensitive layer (the retina) at the back of the eye. Nerve impulses, generated in sensory neurones of the optic nerve, are transmitted to the visual centres of the cortex of the cerebral hemispheres, where they are interpreted as pictures.

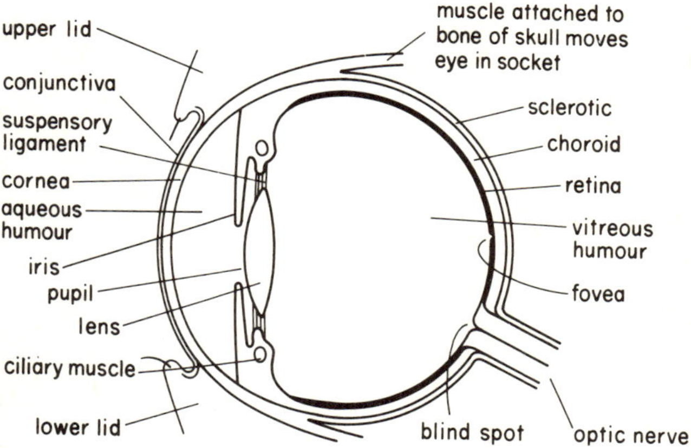

Fig. 9.7 *Cross-section human eye*

Functions of parts of the eye

1 **Eyelids** – protect the eye. Reflex blinking spreads secretions of tear glands evenly over surface and cleans surface.
2 **Tear glands** – secrete watery fluid (tears) which flows over the surface of the eye and is drained into the nasal cavity.
3 **Conjunctiva** – thin, transparent layer protecting the cornea.
4 **Sclerotic** – tough protective layer forming the white of the eye where it is exposed at the front.
5 **Cornea** – transparent disc of tissue in the front part of the sclerotic. Allows light to enter the eye and is the main region of focusing light in the eye.

6 **Choroid** – well-vascularized, darkly pigmented layer that prevents internal reflection.
7 **Aqueous** and **vitreous humours** – fluids that maintain the spherical shape of the eye (keep it turgid). They also play a part in focusing light. The watery aqueous humour moves slowly across the lens, supplying it with nutrients and oxygen and removing waste products. Vitreous humour is jelly-like.
8 **Lens** – composed of transparent living tissue. Convex in shape, it focuses light to a sharp image on the retina. It is elastic and contractions of the ciliary muscles alter its shape and therefore its focal length (**accommodation**).
9 **Iris** – a ring of circular and radial smooth muscle which, by contracting, can alter the size of the hole (**pupil**) in the centre and therefore control the amount of light entering the eye. When the circular muscle fibres contract the pupil gets smaller; this happens in bright light and when viewing near objects. When the radial muscle fibres contract, the pupil gets larger (in dim light and when viewing distant objects).
10 **Retina** – light-sensitive cells on which image is focused.
11 **Rods** – sensitive to low light intensities but do not detect colour. Responsible for what is known as 'twilight' vision.
12 **Cones** – sensitive to bright light and colours. Concentrated in the region known as the fovea (central depression), the centre of normal daylight vision, producing a sharp image.
13 **Blind spot** – point on retina where optic nerve leaves the eye. No rods or cones here and therefore no vision.

Focusing of light in the eye

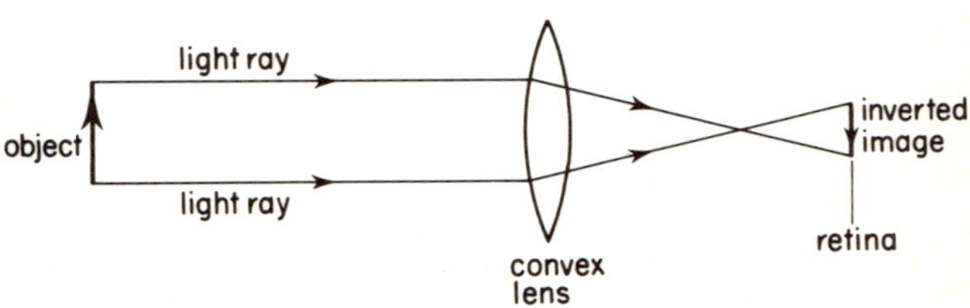

Fig. 9.8 *Focusing light with convex lens*

When light passes from one medium, e.g. air, to another, e.g. cornea, it is **refracted** (bent), resulting in light from object being **focused** to form sharp image on retina. Convex lens of eye produces **inverted** (upside down) image on retina.

1 Most refraction occurs at the cornea. The powers of refraction (focusing) of the lens are less, but it can change shape to bring objects at different distances into focus on the retina (this process is known as accommodation).
2 Eye at rest is **focused on distant objects**. Ciliary muscles are relaxed and suspensory ligaments are tight, pulling the lens thin and flat and decreasing its curvature.
3 When **focusing on a near object** (less than 6 metres) ciliary muscles contract, suspensory ligaments become less taut, elastic lens recoils, becoming fatter and more curved.
4 As a person ages, the lens loses its elasticity and ability to focus on near objects. The nearest point at which the eye can focus on an object (**near point**) gets further away.

Visual defects and their correction

1 **Short sight** (**myopia**) – not able to see **distant** objects clearly.
   - Eyeball too long from front to back; image focused in front of retina.
   - Corrected with concave lenses.

2 **Long sight** (**hypermetropia**) – unable to see **near** objects clearly.
   - Eyeball too short from front to back; image focused beyond retina.
   - Corrected with convex lenses.

The ear

The ear has two functions.

1 **Reception of sound.**
2 **Balance.**

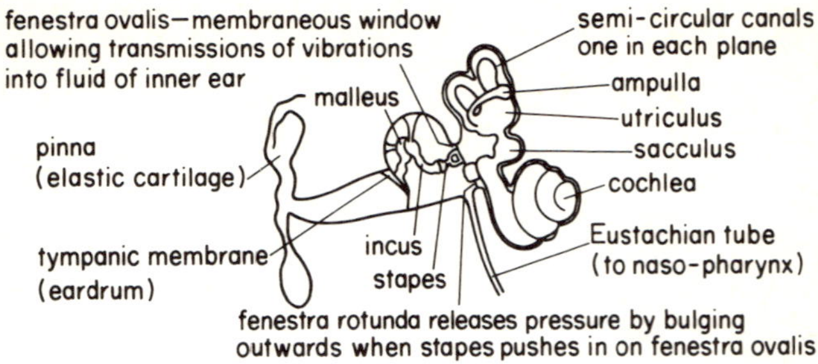

Fig. 9.9 *Human ear*

Outer ear

1 **Pinna** – flexible elastic cartilage. Can be moved by muscles in many mammals to help in sound detection, particularly the direction of the sound.
2 **Ear tube** – S-shaped, leading to the ear drum.
3 **Ear drum** (tympanic membrane) – a sheet of tissue separating the outer ear from the middle ear, caused to vibrate by sound.

Middle ear

Air-filled cavity bridged by three ear bones (**ossicles**) – **malleus**, **incus**, **stapes** – which transmit and amplify vibrations from ear drum. With a very loud noise, reflex contractions of small muscles can dampen down intensity. **Eustachian tube** connects middle ear with pharynx; normally closed, but when swallowing or yawning it opens up and allows equalization of air pressure on either side of tympanic membrane.

Inner ear

Fluid-filled cavity containing membranous system of tubes.
1 **Cochlea** – coiled fluid-filled tube containing organ of Corti.
2 **Organ of Corti** – membranes linked by sensory 'hair' cells; detects sound vibrations, sends nerve impulses to brain.
3 **Semicircular canals, ampullae** – fluid filled, involved in balance.

The ear and sound detection

1 Sound waves enter outer ear and travel to ear drum.
2 Ear drum is vibrated by sound waves in the air.
3 Malleus, incus and stapes are vibrated by ear drum.
4 Stapes vibrates membrane of the fenestra ovalis.
5 Fenestra ovalis vibrates fluid in inner ear.
6 The fluid vibrates the membranes of the cochlea.
7 Sensory 'hair' cells of the organ of Corti are stimulated.
8 This causes a stream of nerve impulses to pass along the auditory nerve to hearing centres in cortex of cerebral hemispheres of brain, to be interpreted as 'hearing'.

The ear and balance

1 There are three semicircular canals, one in each plane.
2 They are fluid filled, with a swelling at one end (**ampulla**).
3 Ampullae have sensory 'hair' cells, embedded in gelatinous mucus, which can detect movements of the fluid.
4 If the head is **rotated** in any direction:
   - ⋆ the fluid lags behind the movement of the canals for a fraction of a second;
   - ⋆ the 'hair' cells in the ampullae are bent as they are pulled through the fluid;
   - ⋆ the bending of the 'hair' cells initiates a stream of nerve impulses in nerves leading to balance centres in cerebellum of brain, where they are interpreted and reflex action taken to counteract any imbalance if necessary.

5 If the head is **tilted** from the vertical:
   - ⋆ gelatinous masses with sensory 'hair' cells bend due to gravity;
   - ⋆ the bending of the 'hair' cells initiates a stream of nerve impulses to balance centres in cerebellum of brain, and reflex action is taken to correct any imbalance if necessary.

10 THE ENDOCRINE SYSTEM

This system consists of endocrine or **ductless glands** (as opposed to exocrine glands which have ducts, e.g. salivary glands). Endocrine glands produce chemicals (**hormones**), secreted directly into the bloodstream. Hormones, although only produced in small amounts, have a powerful effect on the body and its functions, controlling and coordinating activities.

1 Maintaining homeostasis, i.e. constant internal conditions, e.g. osmoregulation, blood sugar, blood calcium, etc.
2 Regulating long-term growth and development.
3 Controlling rhythmic body cycles, e.g. reproductive cycles, and seasonal cycles of activity, e.g. hibernation.
4 Coordinating body systems to act together in an emergency.
5 Controlling sequences of events and coordinating them with requirements, e.g. hormonal control of digestive juices.

Hormones are a chemically mixed group, e.g. some are proteins, some steroids, some are rapidly broken down, some are not. Some hormones are antagonistic, e.g. insulin decreases blood sugar, adrenaline increases it. Homeostasis results from the balance between two such opposing hormones.

Coordination of the endocrine system

Although consisting of scattered glands and patches of tissue throughout the body, the endocrine system is coordinated by:

1 autonomic nervous system, both directly and via hypothalamus, with its direct connections with pituitary gland;
2 negative feedback of hormone levels – secretion of two hormones controlled by level of each hormone in blood circulating between two glands, e.g.

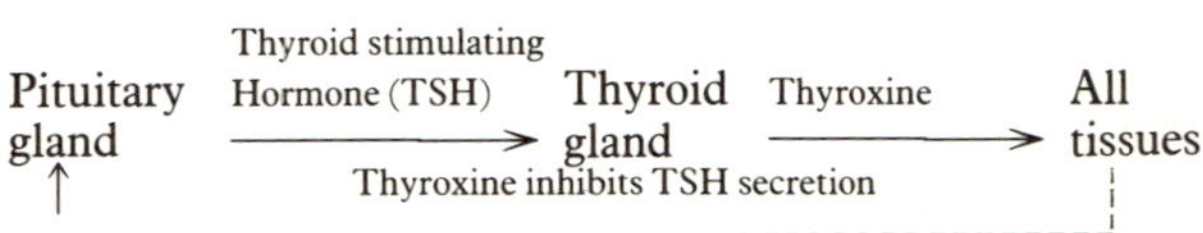

- ★ Thyroxine high ⟶ TSH low.
- ★ TSH low ⟶ Thyroxine low.
- ★ Thyroxine low ⟶ TSH high.
- ★ TSH high ⟶ Thyroxine high.

The main endocrine glands in man

Pituitary

The 'master' gland (has connection with brain) secreting:

1 hormones that control other endocrine glands:
   * **thyroid stimulating hormone** (TSH);
   * **adrenal cortex stimulating hormone;**
   * **gonadotrophic hormones** control reproductive organs;

2 hormones that affect parts of the body directly:
   * **anti-diuretic hormone** (ADH) decreases the amount of water lost in the urine from the kidneys;
   * **growth hormone** stimulates overall growth;
   * hormone that stimulates contraction of uterus at birth.

Thyroid

Secretes **thyroxine** which:

1 stimulates metabolism;
2 is necessary for physical and mental development.

Patches of endocrine cells in the pancreas

Secrete **insulin** which decreases level of blood sugar by:

1 increasing the conversion of glucose to glycogen;
2 increasing the use of glucose by the tissues.

Adrenal glands

1 **Adrenal cortex** secretes hormones controlling salt balance.

2 **Adrenal medulla** secretes **adrenaline** which prepares body for emergencies by increasing:
   * heart rate and therefore blood flow to muscles;
   * breathing rate and therefore oxygen level in blood;
   * blood sugar by conversion of glycogen to glucose.

Gonads

1 **Ovaries** in female secretes:
   * **oestrogen** – controls secondary sexual characteristics,

development of egg, prepares uterus for pregnancy;

- ⋆ **progesterone** – maintains pregnancy if it occurs.

2 **Testes** in male secrete **testosterone** – controls secondary sexual characteristics and development of sperm.

11 REPRODUCTION

Reproduction is a characteristic of all living things. It may be **asexual** or **sexual**.

Asexual reproduction

1 Only one parent organism is involved.
2 It does not involve the fusion of cells.
3 It involves a process of nuclear division (**mitosis**), in which there is no halving of the chromosome number.
4 All offspring are genetically identical to the parent and to each other. There is **no** genetic variation.

Methods of asexual reproduction

1 **Binary fission** – seen in single-celled organisms, e.g. bacteria, and many protozoa, e.g. *Amoeba*. Nucleus divides in two and cytoplasm cleaves into two halves, producing two new 'daughter' cells.
2 **Budding** (in animals) – seen in simpler animals, e.g. *Hydra*. Rapid cell division in a certain area gives rise to small version of the adult which breaks away.
3 **Spore formation** – seen typically in bacteria and plants. Characteristic of parasitic and saprophytic microorganisms, e.g. bacteria and fungi, where production of vast numbers of easily-dispersed spores is necessary to reach new food sources. Spores are single cells with a resistant coat, typically produced in sporangia, e.g. fungi, mosses, ferns.
4 **Vegetative reproduction** (propagation) – seen in plants where a part of the parent body separates to form a new individual (see page 98).

Sexual reproduction

1 Involves fusion of two sex cells (**gametes**) in fertilization.
2 May involve two single-sexed individuals (male and female).
3 May involve one self-fertilizing **hermaphrodite** individual (with both male and female sex organs), or two hermaphrodites cross-fertilizing.

4 Involves **meiosis** – chromosome number halved.
5 Meiosis and fertilization result in **genetic variation** in young.

Meiosis

In animals and higher plants the body cells have two sets of chromosomes (**diploid** or $2n$). In meiosis the chromosome number is halved, resulting in gametes with only one set of chromosomes (**haploid** or n). Thus the diploid number is restored at fertilization, the offspring having the same number of chromosomes as the parents.

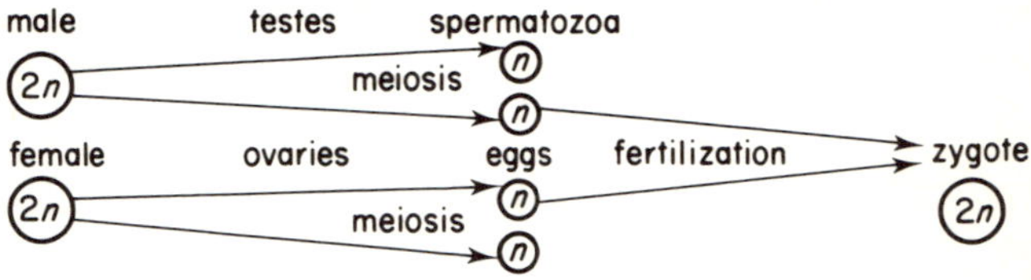

Fig. 11.1 *Meiosis and fertilization in humans*

Gametes

Gametes or sex cells that fuse in fertilization may look similar, e.g. as in *Mucor* and *Spirogyra*. Typically, however, the male gametes are small and motile, while the female gametes (egg cells) are larger (containing food reserves), and non-motile.

Fertilization

The fusion of **two haploid gametes** to form a single cell – the **diploid zygote**. Hermaphrodite organisms may either be self-fertilizing, e.g. some flowering plants, or cross-fertilizing, e.g. earthworm, most flowering plants. Organisms with separate sexes (male and female) are always cross-fertilizing, i.e. zygote contains a combination of genetic material from the two parents and therefore shows genetic variation from parents. Meiosis results in all gametes produced by an individual being genetically different; offspring thus show genetic variation from each other as well as from parents. Fertilization also stimulates development of zygote into new individual.

Fertilization may be **external** (gametes released outside the parents' bodies) as in many aquatic organisms, e.g. *Hydra*, many fish, or **internal** (fertilization of female gametes within female parent) as in most terrestrial and many aquatic organisms.

Mammalian reproduction

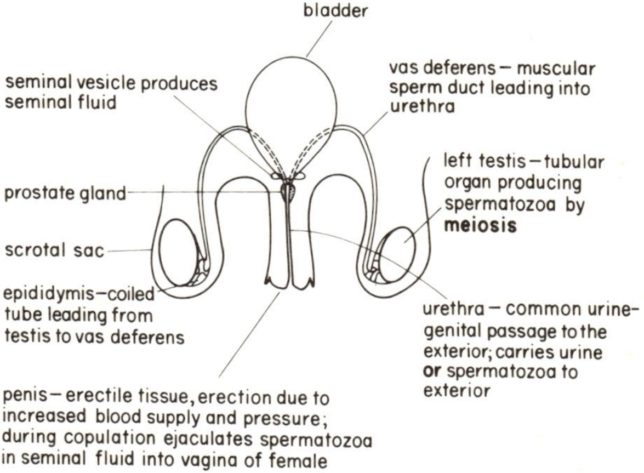

Fig. 11.2 *Ventral view, male reproductive system*

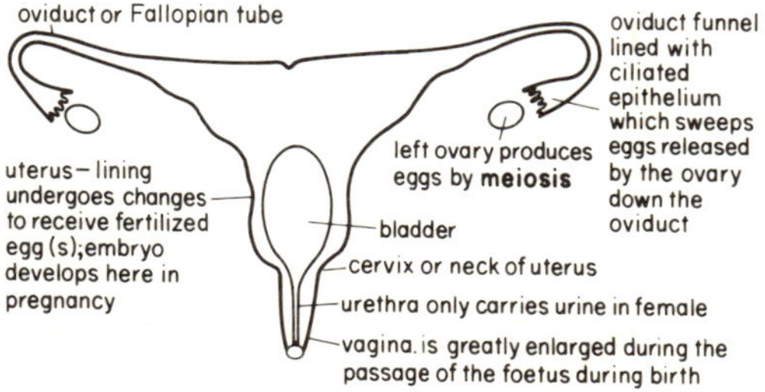

Fig. 11.3 *Ventral view, female reproductive system*

Fertilization

As a result of copulation, several million spermatozoa in seminal fluid are ejaculated by the erect penis into the vagina and use their flagella to swim towards the oviduct. The ovaries release eggs which are moved down the oviduct by cilia lining the oviduct wall. Fertilization usually occurs high up in the oviduct. One sperm penetrates an egg and their haploid nuclei fuse to form a diploid fertilized egg or **zygote**.

Development of the zygote

Immediately after fertilization the zygote begins to divide to form a ball of cells as it moves down the oviduct. On entering the uterus it embeds in the uterus wall which is thickened and vascularized for its reception. The ball of cells develops rapidly into an embryo surrounded by protective embryonic membranes (amnion). Placenta develops and becomes main organ of attachment and exchange between embryo and mother.

Placenta

The placenta has a large surface area for exchange by diffusion between the bloodstream of the embryo and the mother. The embryo receives oxygen, water and nutrients and rids itself of carbon dioxide, urea and other waste products. The two circulations should not mix as the maternal blood pressure is too high, maternal antibodies would attack the embryo, maternal waste products would be toxic and maternal hormones would be incompatible with the embryo.

Birth

After a period of development (**gestation** – about 40 weeks in humans) birth occurs under the stimulus and control of reproductive hormones. The uterus wall starts strong rhythmic contractions, the cervix relaxes and widens and the embryo is pushed head first into the vagina and from the mother's body. The baby is still attached to the placenta by the umbilical cord, which must be severed; the placenta (**afterbirth**) is then expelled. The young are suckled with milk from the mother's mammary glands. The milk contains necessary nutrients, and antibodies against certain infections.

Female reproductive hormones

At the onset of sexual maturity (**puberty**) the **pituitary gland** (attached to the brain) secretes hormones which stimulate the ovaries to secrete their own hormones and to release eggs at intervals. The ovaries secrete:

1 **oestrogen** – stimulates the development of:
- ⋆ primary sexual characteristics (reproductive system);
- ⋆ secondary sexual characteristics (development of breasts, body hair, hip girdle enlargement, emotions);
- ⋆ lining of uterus for reception of fertilized egg;

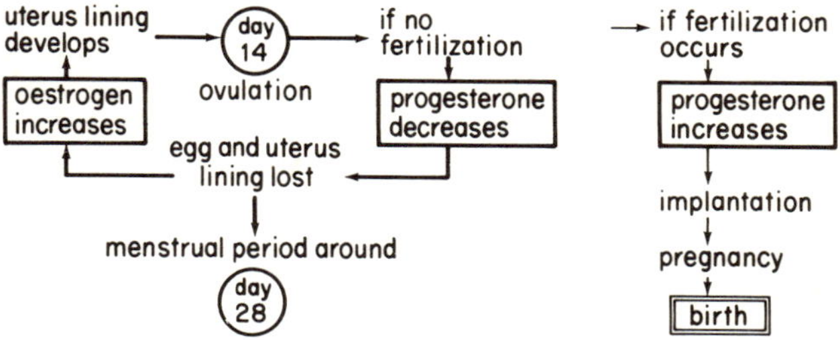

Fig. 11.4 *Hormones of the ovary*

2 **progesterone** (secreted after ovulation):
- ⋆ maintains development of uterus lining and other conditions necessary for pregnancy;
- ⋆ stops the release of any more eggs.

If fertilization **does** occur, pregnancy is maintained by continued secretion of progesterone. If fertilization does **not** occur, progesterone secretion drops, uterus lining breaks down and is eliminated as menstrual (monthly) flow about 14 days after the release of egg by an ovary (**ovulation**). Oestrogen increases, lining of uterus re-develops, another egg is released and cycle is repeated (taking about 28 days – **menstrual cycle**).

Male reproductive hormones

At puberty the testes secrete testosterone which stimulates primary sexual characteristics, as well as secondary sexual characteristics of body, e.g. facial hair, larger larynx (deeper voice), muscular physique, less body fat, emotions.

Reproduction in flowering plants (reference to sweet pea)

Flowers contain the reproductive organs of flowering plants; pollination and fertilization result in seeds and fruits. The flower parts are arranged in rings on the receptacle: the outer ring is the calyx of sepals; next the corolla of petals; then the androecium of stamens; finally the gynoecium of carpels.

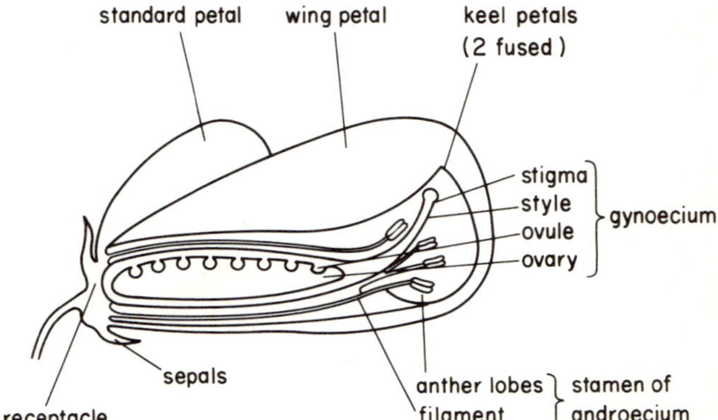

Fig. 11.5 *LS sweet pea flower*

1 **Calyx** – 5 sepals, green scale-like structures, protect bud.
2 **Corolla** – 5 brightly coloured petals of different shapes, designed for insect pollination.
3 **Androecium** – 10 stamens, male part of flower. Each stamen consist of a filament and anther lobes containing pollen sacs which produce pollen grains containing male gametes.
4 **Gynoecium** – 1 carpel, female part of flower. Stigma receives pollen grains in pollination and style leads to ovary containing ovules containing female gametes.

Flowers of most plants have both stamens and carpels, i.e. they are bisexual or hermaphrodite. Some plants have flowers which are either male or female; some have both male and female flowers on same plant, e.g. hazel. Others have separate male plants with male flowers and female plants with female flowers, e.g. holly, stinging nettles, willows.

Pollination

This is the transfer of pollen from anthers to stigma. If this occurs in one flower it is self-pollination; if it occurs between different flowers of plants of same species it is cross-pollination (true of most plants).

Characteristics of insect-pollinated flowers

1 Petals brightly coloured and scented to attract insects.
2 Nectaries secrete nectar to attract insects which feed on it; in sweet pea, nectar can only be reached by insects with long mouthparts, e.g. bees. Some insect-pollinated flowers do not have nectaries, e.g. lupin, gorse, broom.
3 Arrangement of petals 'fits' insect; in sweet pea a bee lands on keel, its weight pushes it down and anthers and stigmas stick up and touch underside of bee. Sweet pea stamens mature before stigma, so cross-pollination occurs.
4 Pollen grains – large, rough and sticky to stick to insect.

Characteristics of wind-pollinated flowers

1 Small flowers, small petals often green or even absent.
2 No scent or nectaries – no need to attract insects.

3 Flowers often appear before leaves – helps exposure to wind.
4 Large anthers with long filaments so they hang in the wind.
5 Pollen grains are small, smooth, 'dust'-like, so they blow in the wind. Large amounts produced to ensure pollination.
6 Stigmas are large and 'feathery' – well-exposed to wind.
7 Most have stamens and carpels maturing at different times.
8 Examples – grasses, oak, beech, ash, elm, hazel, dock.

Pollen grain development

When a pollen grain lands on the stigma it is nourished by a sugary solution secreted by the stigma. A pollen tube grows down between the cells of the style, secreting enzymes which digest the tissue of the style, and absorbs nutrients. It enters an ovule through a small pore (**micropyle**). The development of the pollen tube is controlled by a pollen tube nucleus which eventually disintegrates. The pollen tube also contains a **male nucleus** which fertilizes a **female nucleus** in the ovule.

Fertilization

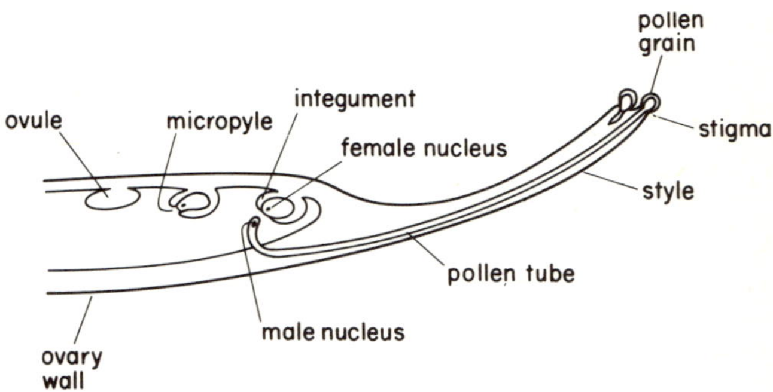

Fig. 11.6 *Fertilization in sweet pea*

The pollen tube tip breaks down and the **haploid male nucleus** fuses with **haploid female egg cell nucleus** in ovule to form

diploid zygote. Each ovule is fertilized by one pollen grain. Fertilization triggers seed and fruit formation.

Fruit

After fertilization, changes occur in flower to produce fruit, which contain seeds; sepals, petals, stigma and style wither.

1 **True fruit** develop from ovary, ovary wall forming fruit wall or pericarp.
2 **False fruit** (**pseudocarps**) develop from some other part, e.g. receptacle in apples and strawberries.
3 Fruit play important part in protection and dispersal of seeds.

Outline classification of types of fruit

1 **Dry fruits** have a dry fruit wall (pericarp).
- ⋆ **Indehiscent** dry fruit contain one seed; do not have special mechanism for releasing it, e.g. buttercup, oak.
- ⋆ **Dehiscent** dry fruit contain many seeds; have special mechanisms for release, e.g. sweet pea, lupin, poppy.

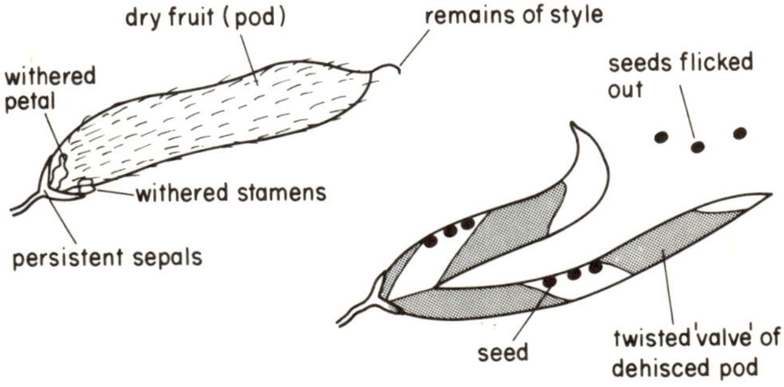

Fig. 11.7 *Dehiscence of sweet pea pod*

2 **Succulent fruits** have a juicy fruit wall, e.g. tomato, blackberry, grape, cherry.

Dispersal

1 **Mechanical dispersal** – seeds flicked or pushed out by action

of fruit wall, e.g. sweet-pea (and all leguminous plants, e.g. peas, beans, lupins, etc.) fruit is a dry pod which splits open and twists as it dries, flicking seeds out.

2 **Wind dispersal** – wind-dispersed fruits and seeds tend to be light with large surface area. Some have large wing-shaped pericarp, e.g. elm, sycamore, ash; others have 'parachute' of hairy filaments to catch the wind, e.g. dandelion, willowherb. clematis.

3 **Censer dispersal** – ovary becomes a dry hollow capsule, with one or more pores which open when dry. Capsule sways in wind and dust-like seeds are shaken out, e.g. poppy.

4 **Animal dispersal** – juicy, succulent, highly-coloured fruits attract animals which eat them, and in doing so carry the seeds away, either stuck onto their beak, feathers or fur, or via their gut and droppings (some seeds germinate better after testa has been softened by digestive juices), e.g. blackberry, strawberry, cherry, apple. Dry hooked fruits, e.g. goose grass, or seeds, e.g. wood avens, stick to feathers, fur.

5 **Water dispersal** – plants living in or near water may have spongy/fibrous floating fruits, e.g. coconut, or seeds, e.g. water-lily, which are carried away by water currents.

6 **Casual dispersal** – many different types may be dispersed accidentally, e.g. in mud on feet of birds and animals.

Seeds

Fertilized ovules develop into seeds consisting of the following.

1 **Testa** – tough protective coat which enables seeds to withstand adverse conditions and allows seed to lie dormant until conditions are right for germination.

2 **Embryo** – young plant developing from zygote, consisting of:
  * **plumule** – the first shoot;
  * **radicle** – the first root;
  * **cotyledons** – the 'seed' leaves. Most plants have two cotyledons (**dicotyledonous**); others have one (**monocotyledonous**, e.g. grasses, cereals, maize). Cotyledons contain food store, e.g. starch, for developing embryo or utilize food store of another food-storage tissue, the **endosperm**. In some seedlings the cotyledons protect plumule

as it pushes up through soil and act as first photosynthetic leaves when they reach the surface.

3 **Endosperm** – a food storage tissue found only when food is not stored in the cotyledons.

4 **Micropyle** – pore in the testa which allows entry of water at the start of germination.

5 **Hilum** – scar from attachment of seed to fruit wall.

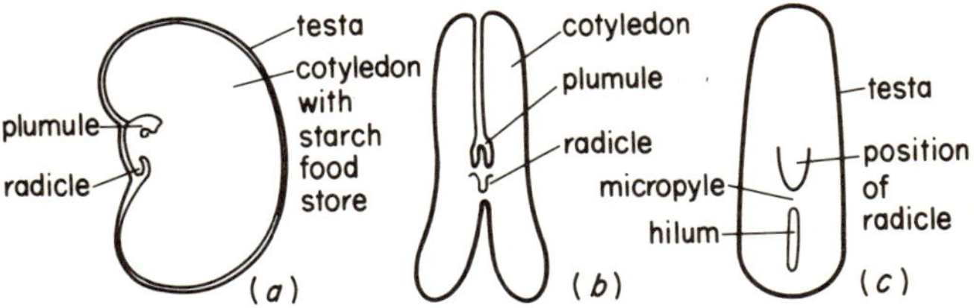

Fig. 11.8 *(a) LS bean seed. (b) Testa removed. (c) Entire seed*

Dormancy

When seeds are dispersed the contents are dry and in an inactive **dormant** state. The testa may contain inhibitors which prevent germination. In this state seeds can be dispersed over long distances and/or can lay in ground until right conditions for germination occur, e.g. many seeds produced in summer or autumn remain dormant until they germinate next spring. Exposure to cold is necessary before certain seeds germinate.

Germination

1 Germination needs:
   * **water**;
   * **oxygen**;
   * **suitable temperature**.

2 **Hydration phase** – the test becomes less waterproof and water enters the seed (through micropyle). The cells enlarge due to absorption of water, cytoplasm becomes active and the enzyme-catalyzed reactions of metabolism begin.

3 **Metabolic phase** – enzyme-catalyzed reactions include conversion of insoluble food reserves, e.g. starch, to soluble

forms, e.g. simple sugars, fatty acids, by hydrolysis. These are transported to actively growing regions of embryo and oxidized in respiration to give energy and/or used for synthesis of new cell materials.

* This enzyme activity has an optimum temperature.
* Aerobic respiration requires a supply of oxygen.

4 As result of cell division and growth, the young seedling eventually bursts through the testa.

Germination of the sweet pea (hypogeal)

1 Radicle emerges first. It is positively geotropic, growing down towards gravity.
2 The tissue behind the radicle (**hypocotyl**) elongates and pushes radicle downwards.
3 Plumule is negatively geotropic and positively phototropic, growing up into a hooked shape to protect the delicate growing point as it is pushed up through the soil by elongation of the tissue behind it (**epicotyl**).
4 Radicle develops into main rooting system, anchoring the plant and absorbing water and salts from soil.
5 Plumule develops chlorophyll and becomes photosynthetic when it reaches the light.
6 Cotyledons shrivel as food reserves are used up.

Epigeal germination

Cotyledons are carried above ground, protecting plumule tip as it pushes through soil. Once in the light, cotyledons turn green and act as first photosynthetic leaves, e.g. sunflower.

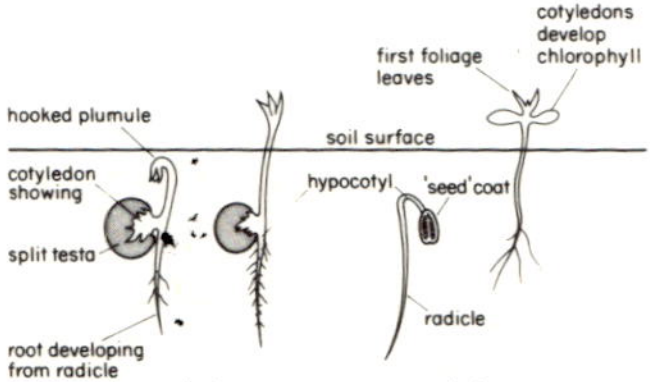

Fig. 11.9 *(a) Hypogeal and (b) epigeal germination*

Vegetative reproduction (propagation)

A type of asexual reproduction involving the separation of some vegetative part of the plant and its development into a new independent plant. It is the main type of reproduction in many flowering plants; often associated with food storage.

1 Less complicated than pollination and fertilization.
2 Problems of fruit and seed production are avoided.
3 Offspring have greater chance of survival; they are virtually fully formed from the start, and often provided with food store by parent plant, allowing rapid and early growth in the spring and early flower and seed formation when necessary.
4 Offspring are genetically identical to parents – there is no variation (good stocks can be easily propagated).
5 Offspring not widely dispersed. This leads to almost complete cover of an area, outcompeting other plants.
6 Food storage organs used as food by man, e.g. potatoes.

Types of vegetative reproduction in flowering plants

1 **Modified roots** – food is stored in fibrous roots which become swollen root tubers. These can separate from parent plant, e.g. dahlia, celandine.
2 **Modified leaves**, e.g. bulbs – underground disc-shaped stem bearing close-set rings of leaves with bases swollen with food reserves; lateral bulbs develop from lateral buds and can separate from parent plant, e.g. daffodil, onion.
3 **Modified stems.**
  ⋆ **Stem tubers** – food stored in swollen tip of underground stems forms stem tubers which separate from parent; new

plants arise from lateral buds ('eyes'), e.g. potato.

- ⋆ **Corms** – swollen base of stem. Corms developing from lateral buds can separate from parent plant, e.g. crocus.
- ⋆ **Rhizomes** – horizontal underground stem which may be swollen with food reserves. New plants arise from lateral branches and fragmentation of parent rhizome, e.g. iris (swollen), and couch grass and mint (not swollen).
- ⋆ **Runners** – horizontal surface stem giving rise at intervals to new plantlets from lateral buds, e.g. strawberry.
- ⋆ **Stolons** – tips of shoots touch the ground, develop adventitious roots, stems and leaves and separate from parent plant, e.g. blackberry.

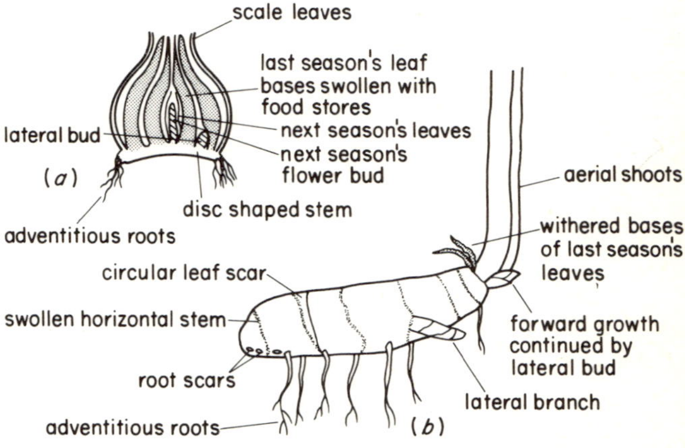

Fig. 11.10 *(a) Daffodil bulb. (b) Iris rhizome*

1 Offspring resemble their parents, but also differ in many ways due to variations in inherited genetic information (**genotype**) and/or environmental influences:
Genotype + Environment = Phenotype (organism as it is)
2 **Genetics** is the study of inheritance and variation.
3 Inherited genetic information is carried in **chromosomes** in the nuclei of cells of organisms.
4 Chromosomes consist of:
- ⋆ genetic material (**DNA**);
- ⋆ **protein**.

5 Chromosomes only become visible just before nuclear division in a dividing cell.
6 There are two types of nuclear division:
- ⋆ **mitosis**;
- ⋆ **meiosis**.

Mitosis

1 Each chromosome forms two **chromatids** before the nucleus divides.
2 Chromatids separate and form new chromosomes.

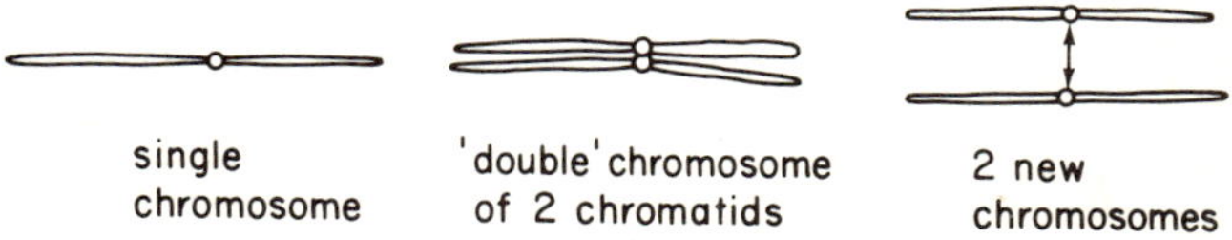

Fig. 12.1 *Chromosome doubling*

3 Thus the nucleus of a cell divides to give two daughter nuclei, each containing the same number of chromosomes as the parent nucleus (the number of chromosomes per cell is constant for any one species, e.g. 46 in man).
4 Daughter cells are genetically identical to parent cell.
5 Mitosis occurs in growth, repair and asexual reproduction.

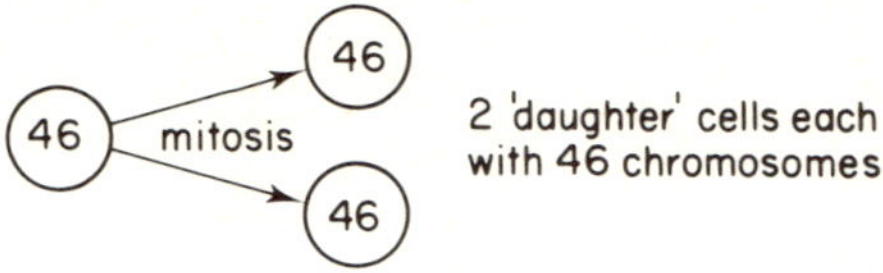

Fig. 12.2 *Mitosis outline for man*

Meiosis

1 Cell nucleus divides to give four daughter cells, each with half the normal chromosome number, e.g. 23 in man.

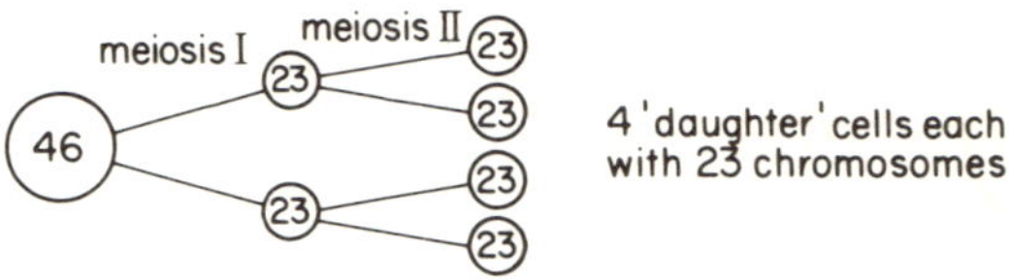

Fig. 12.3 *Meiosis outline for man*

2 This occurs in the formation of sex cells (**gametes**).
3 In man, 23 chromosomes represent one set of chromosomes (**haploid number**).
4 When two haploid gametes fuse in fertilization, a **diploid zygote** is formed containing two sets of chromosomes.
5 This means that in a zygote each chromosome in one set has a partner in the other set, i.e. chromosomes in a diploid nucleus occur in pairs (**homologous pairs**).
6 In meiosis these homologous chromosomes pair up, then repel each other so only one of each pair goes into a gamete.

Significance of meiosis

1 Diploid chromosome number halved to haploid number.
2 The diploid number can thus be restored at fertilization.
3 Crossing over between homologous chromosomes gives genetic variation.

1 Chromosomes carry units of inheritance (**genes**).
2 A diploid nucleus contains pairs of homologous chromosomes. Homologous chromosomes carry genes for the same character in the same positions.

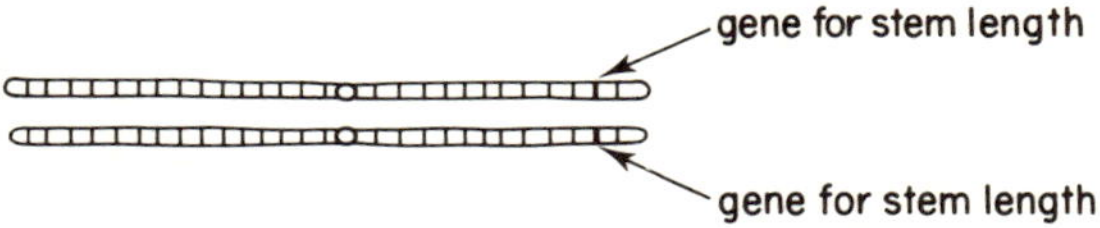

Fig. 12.4 *Homologous chromosomes*

3 These genes can vary slightly, e.g. one may be for a tall stem, the other for a short stem. If the genes are:
- ★ the same the organism is **homozygous** for that character;
- ★ different it is **heterozygous** for that character.

Mendel's experiments

The basic laws of inheritance were discovered by Gregor Mendel (1822–84). His observations can be explained in terms of chromosomes and their behaviour in meiosis and fertilization.

1 He worked with the garden pea, which is normally self-pollinating but can easily be cross-pollinated:
- ★ remove anthers of a flower
- ★ dust pollen from flower of another pea plant onto stigma;
- ★ cover with muslin bag to prevent insects bringing in pollen from other flowers.

2 Chose true-breeding simple pure lines (**homozygous** plants).
3 Pure-breeding tall plants (T gametes) were crossed with pure-breeding short plants (t gametes).
4 Plants grown from the resulting seeds (F_1 generation) were allowed to self-pollinate.
5 The resulting F_2 generation was in the ratio 3 tall : 1 short.

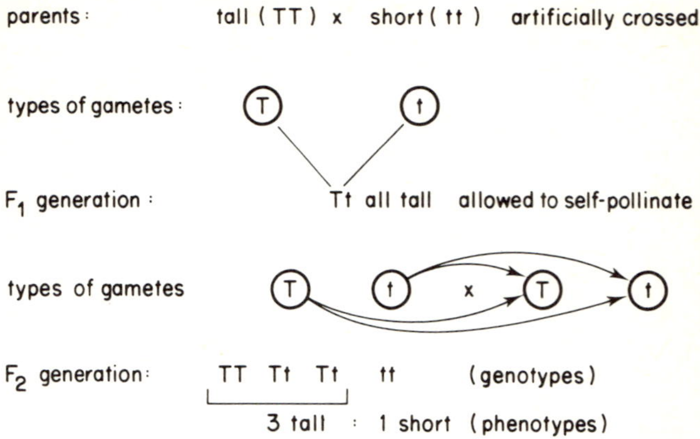

Fig. 12.5 *Mendel's experiment with garden peas*

6 Conclusions.
- ⋆ Tall is **dominant** to short.
- ⋆ Short is **recessive** to tall.
- ⋆ For a recessive character to show it must be homozygous for the recessive gene.

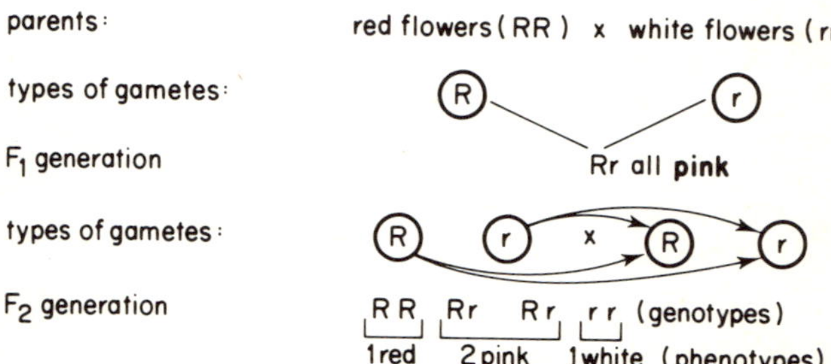

Fig. 12.6 *Incomplete dominance*

Incomplete dominance

In some cases neither of a pair of characters is dominant to another. They are said to be **co-dominant** or to show **incomplete dominance**; the heterozygous individuals show a 'blending' of the two features.

Sex determination in mammals

1 An individual's sex is determined genetically by a pair of special sex chromosomes.
- ⋆ Females have two **X** chromosomes.
- ⋆ Males have one **X** chromosome and one **Y** chromosome.

Fig. 12.7 *Sex chromosomes in (a) male (b) female*

2 The sex chromosomes pair and separate at meiosis.
3 There is thus an equal chance of a male or a female being produced as a result of fertilization, giving roughly equal numbers of males and females in the population as a whole.

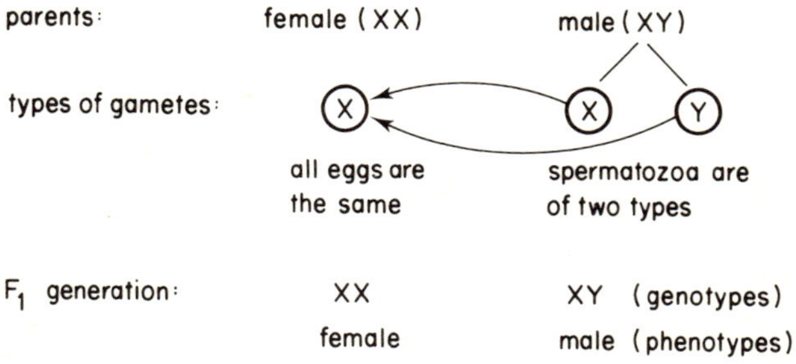

Fig. 12.8 *Sex determination in mammals*

Sex-linked characteristics

1 As well as being involved in sex determination, the X chromosome carries other genes.

2 The characteristics determined by these genes are said to be **sex-linked**, i.e. their pattern of inheritance is linked to the pattern of sex inheritance.

3 **Y** chromosome does *not* carry sex-linked genes, so any recessive sex-linked genes on **X** chromosome will show up in phenotype of male, i.e. single recessive sex-linked gene will show up in male.

4 For a recessive sex-linked gene to show up in the phenotype of the female it must be present on **both** X chromosomes.

- ⋆ Single recessive sex-linked gene will not show in female.
- ⋆ Female with single recessive sex-linked gene is a **carrier**.
- ⋆ Less chance of a female showing a recessive sex-linked trait as this would require two copies (**alleles**) of the recessive gene, one on each of the two X chromosomes.

5 Examples – haemophilia and red-green colour blindness.

- ⋆ **Haemophilia** – blood clotting is disrupted.
- ⋆ Controlled by a recessive gene (h) on X chromosome.
- ⋆ Single dose females are carriers.
- ⋆ Single dose males suffer from disease (haemophilia).
- ⋆ Double dose females are still-born.
- ⋆ Although male haemophiliacs rarely live long enough to have children and female haemophiliacs are still-born, haemophilia remains present at a steady level in population because new cases arise by **mutation**.

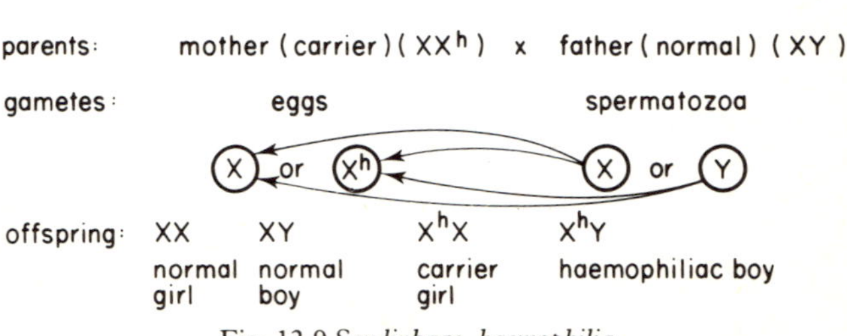

Fig. 12.9 *Sex linkage, haemophilia*

Variation

Variation in offspring of reproduction can be one of two types.

1 **Discontinuous variations** are those that:
   - ⋆ show distinct differences from one another;
   - ⋆ have no range of intermediates;
   - ⋆ are only affected to a limited extent by the environment;
   - ⋆ are usually controlled by a single gene.
   - ⋆ **Examples**: blood groups, eye colour, flower colour.

2 **Continuous variations** are those that:
   - ⋆ do not show clearly defined differences from one another;
   - ⋆ do have a range of intermediates;
   - ⋆ are affected by the environment, e.g. diet;
   - ⋆ are usually controlled by several genes.
   - ⋆ **Examples**: height and weight.

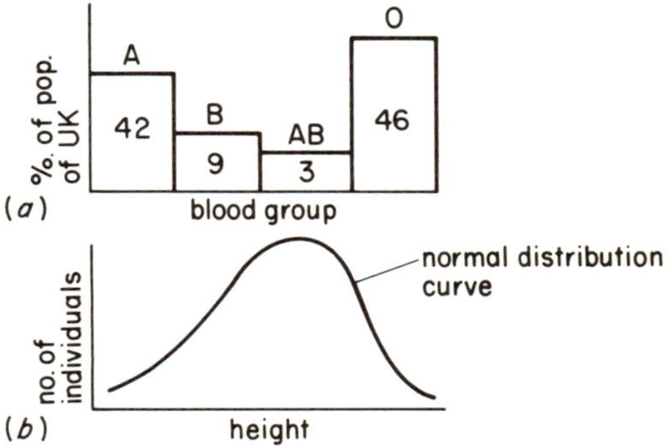

Fig. 12.10 *(a) Discontinuous and (b) continuous variation*

Evolution

Variation in the offspring is thought to be the 'raw material' of evolution. Darwin and Wallace (1858) formulated the theory of natural selection to explain how species may evolve.

1 Offspring vary from their parents and from each other.
2 More offspring are born than survive.
3 There is a struggle for existence.

4 Only the best adapted (the fittest) survive to reproduce.
5 Favourable variations are passed on to the offspring.
6 Isolated populations can become sufficiently different to form a new species unable to interbreed with original species.

13 SOIL

Soil is a complex mixture of the following.

1 **Sand** – large particles (2.0–0.02 mm) of silica dioxide. Due to size and angular shape they do not pack tightly together, so have large air spaces between them. Sand particles do not hold water very strongly, so sandy soils drain rapidly and contain much air.

2 **Clay** – small particles (0.002 mm and less) of complex chemical composition. Due to size and round shape they pack together tightly, with small air spaces between in which water is held by capillary action. Particles also attract water strongly, so clay soils hold much water (easily waterlogged) but contain little air. Clay particles are rich in plant nutrients, and attract ions to their surface, preventing them being washed away (**leached**).

3 **Humus** – decomposing dead organic matter that forms a dark sticky mass in the soil. It is important to soil fertility:
   - ⋆ the main source of plant nutrients in the soil;
   - ⋆ binds clay particles into small lumps (crumbs) which improve aeration and drainage of heavy clay soils;
   - ⋆ helps retain water in light dry sandy soils and prevents nutrients from being leached away by rain water;
   - ⋆ dark colour means it absorbs much heat from the sun.

4 **Soil organisms** play an essential part in soil fertility.
   - ⋆ Microorganisms (bacteria and fungi) **decompose** dead organic matter, breaking it down and releasing nutrients, e.g. nitrates, for uptake by roots of plants.
   - ⋆ Earthworms burrow through soil, improve aeration and drainage, break down organic matter and mix it with soil.

Composition and characteristics of fertile loam soil

A cultivated soil of good composition and fertility is known as a **loam**. A loam soil consists of about 50% sand, 30% clay, 20% humus and sufficient calcium carbonate to ensure that the soil is neither too acid nor too alkaline (pH 7). It will have a good stable structure, with sufficient air and water to promote the healthy growth of roots and the many soil organisms.

Soil experiments

1 To determine the amount of water in a soil.
  - ⋆ Heat known weight of soil for an hour at about 100°C.
  - ⋆ Cool in a desiccator and re-weigh.
  - ⋆ Repeat until no further loss of weight.
  - ⋆ Difference between original weight and dry soil gives weight of water originally present in soil sample.
  - ⋆ Weight of water/Original weight of soil × 100 = Water content (%).

2 To determine the amount of humus in a soil.
  - ⋆ Heat known weight of dry soil in crucible until black charred organic matter has burnt off (no more smoke).
  - ⋆ Cool in desiccator and re-weigh.
  - ⋆ Loss in weight = Weight of humus in dry soil sample.
  - ⋆ Weight of humus/Original weight of dry soil × 100 = Humus content (%).

3 To investigate water-holding properties of a soil.
  - ⋆ Plug three filter funnels with equal amounts of glass wool and half-fill with dried, powdered and sieved sand, clay and loam respectively.
  - ⋆ Measured amount of water poured onto surface of soils.
  - ⋆ Water that drains through is collected and measured.
  - ⋆ Volume of water poured on − Volume of water collected = Volume of water held by soil.

4 To investigate the rate of drainage through soils.
  - ⋆ Use three funnels of damp soil from previous experiment.
  - ⋆ Pour 2–3 cm water on top of each sample.
  - ⋆ Keep water topped up to this level – keeps constant weight of water acting down through soil.
  - ⋆ Volume of water draining through in specific time gives rate of drainage.

5 To demonstrate the effect of lime on clay particles, a cloudy suspension of clay particles will clear when slaked lime is added. The clay particles are clumped together (**flocculated**) and settle out of suspension.

Air pollution

1 **Sulphur dioxide** (SO_2) is released into the air as a result of burning coal and oil, especially from power stations, and is washed out of the air by rain. Sulphur dioxide dissolves in the rain forming sulphuric acid, i.e. 'acid' rain. 'Acid' rain dissolves important mineral salts from the soil, decreasing soil fertility and washing them into rivers and lakes. Acid rivers and lakes cannot support life and become sterile. 'Acid' rain is threatening the forests and waters of Europe.

2 **Smoke and grit** are also released into the air as a result of burning coal and oil. They cover leaves, reducing photosynthesis, and can cause lung irritation and disease in man.

3 **Carbon dioxide** is released by combustion, including the combustion of petrol in cars. The level of carbon dioxide in the air is rising and the long-term effects of this are being studied.

4 **Carbon monoxide** is released in car exhausts and found in tobacco smoke. It combines irreversibly with haemoglobin in the blood to form stable carboxyhaemoglobin, preventing the carriage of oxygen as oxyhaemoglobin.

5 **Tobacco smoke** is the most intense and harmful form of local air pollution, to smokers and non-smokers alike.

Water pollution

1 **Sulphur dioxide** – as discussed above.

2 **Nitrates** from nitrate fertilizers washed from the soil by rain, and in sewage effluent. Nitrates cause over-fertilizing of water so that algae grow too rapidly and the web of life is disrupted.

3 **Pesticides and herbicides** – poisonous chemicals sprayed onto land and crops are washed out of the soil by rain and reach lakes and rivers and, eventually, the sea. They become concentrated in animals at the top of food chains, e.g. carnivores, accumulate high levels of poisonous chemicals in their tissues. The discovery of DDT in high concentrations in animals all over the world led to it being banned.

15 VARIETY OF LIFE

It is necessary to attempt to classify organisms into groups:

1 so that every organism can be placed in an ordered system, for ease of reference whenever required;
2 to reveal possible relationships between different groups of organisms, from the simple to the complex;
3 to establish a consistent scientific name for every organism.

Classification

The classification of organisms is based mainly on structure, although their ability to interbreed, and many other features, are also important. The smallest grouping in the system is the **species**. Members of the same species usually:

1 resemble each other more than members of other species;
2 interbreed to produce fertile offspring;
3 do not interbreed with members of other species; if they do they do not produce fertile offspring.

Groups of similar species are placed in same **genus**. Every organism is given a two-word name (**binomial system**); the first is the name of its genus, the second the name of its species, e.g. *Lumbricus terrestris* (earthworm), *Hydra viridis* (hydra), *Fagus sylvatica* (beech tree). There is a series of larger and larger groupings up to the **phylum**, e.g. all unicellular animals are placed in the phylum Protozoa.

Plant kingdom – main groups

Algae

Simple, aquatic; photosynthetic with chlorophyll; some unicellular, some very large seaweeds; wide range of forms; e.g. *Spirogyra*, *Chlamydomonas*, *Fucus* and *Sargassum* (seaweeds).

Fungi

Lack chlorophyll so non-photosynthetic, therefore saprophytes or parasites; filaments or hyphae make up plant body or mycelium; reproduction by spores; e.g. *Mucor* (mould), mushrooms and toadstools, yeast.

Mosses and liverworts (bryophytes)
Terrestrial, aquatic; green plant has rhizoids (not roots), stem and simple leaf-like structures; main plant is haploid gametophyte generation bearing sex organs; sexual reproduction produces diploid sporophyte growing on parent plant; sporophyte produce spores by meiosis; spores are haploid, grow into another haploid gametophyte plant (alternation of generations); e.g. *Sphagnum* (bog moss), *Funaria* (common moss), *Pellia* (liverwort).

Ferns (pteridophytes)
Alternation of generations; haploid gametophyte small green plant; diploid sporophyte large main plant with roots, stems and leaves; produce spores on leaves; e.g. ferns, *Pteridium* (bracken).

Conifers (gymnosperms)
Trees; reproductive structures are cones; male cones produce pollen, female cones produce seeds on top of scales, i.e. 'naked' seeds; no flowers or fruits; e.g. *Pinus* (pine).

Flowering plants (angiosperms)
Wide range of forms, from herbs to shrubs and trees; reproductive structures are flowers; seeds produced inside ovaries which develop into fruits, i.e. 'covered' seeds; e.g. *Primula* (primrose), *Quercus* (oak tree).

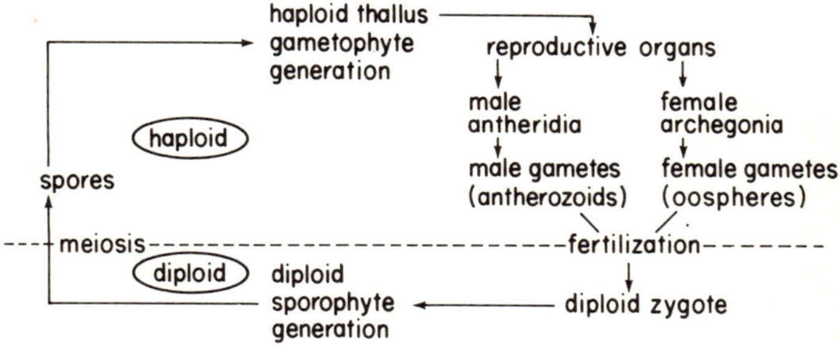

Fig. 15.1 *Alternation of generations in plants*

Animal kingdom – main groups

Animal kingdom consists of two major groups:

1 **invertebrates** – without a 'backbone';
2 **vertebrates** – with a 'backbone'.

Invertebrates

1 **Protozoa** – unicellular, microscopic, aquatic, e.g. *Amoeba*, *Paramecium*, *Euglena*, *Plasmodium* (malarial parasite).
2 **Coelenterates** – multicellular; have tissues; two-layered body wall (**diploblastic**); simple body cavity (**coelenteron**) with single opening mouth; tentacles with sting cells; radially symmetrical; coelenterates are typically marine and colonial; e.g. *Actinia* (sea anemone), *Aurelia* (jellyfish), *Hydra* (solitary, freshwater).
3 **Platyhelminthes** (flatworms) – flat body shape; most parasites of vertebrates with invertebrate secondary host; e.g. *Taenia* (tapeworm), *Fasciola* (fluke), *Planaria* (aquatic).
4 **Nematodes** (roundworms) – elongated cylindrical body; gut a simple tube with two openings, the mouth and anus; sexes usually separate; many of the nematodes are parasitic; e.g. *Ascaris* (common gut roundworm), *Toxacara* (dog and cat roundworm).
5 **Annelids** (segmented worms) – have a body cavity in the mesoderm (the **coelom**), associated with an overall increase in size and complexity; body is **metamerically segmented** into a series of similar segments; bristle-like chaetae; e.g. *Nereis* (ragworm), *Lumbricus* (earthworm). (All animals, from the annelids upwards, are coelomate and metamerically segmented, including man, although the pattern of segmentation can be obscured by specialization.)
6 **Arthropods** – strong exoskeleton; flexible joints; growth requires moulting (**ecdysis**); largest phylum (80% of all species).
   - ⋆ **Class Crustacea** – aquatic; two pairs of antennae; respire with gills; exoskeleton expanded to form a dorsal shield (**carapace**); e.g. *Carcinus* (common shore crab), *Daphnia* (water flea).
   - ⋆ **Class Insecta** – head, thorax and abdomen; three pairs of

walking legs attached to thorax; typically two pairs of wings attached to thorax; waterproof exoskeleton; metamorphosis in life cycle; more than 50% of known species of animals are insects; e.g. beetles, butterflies, moths, flies, mosquitoes, etc.

- ⋆ **Class Arachnida** – body divided in two; four pairs of legs; e.g. spiders, mites, ticks.
- ⋆ **Class Myriapoda** – many pairs of walking legs; e.g. centipedes, millipedes.

7 **Molluscs** – head, visceral mass and muscular foot; typically have a shell although may be absent; e.g. *Helix* (common garden snail), *Limax* (slug), mussels, squid.

8 **Echinoderms** – spiny; radially symmetrical; marine; e.g. *Asterias* (starfish), *Echinus* (sea-urchin).

Vertebrates

1 **Pisces** (fish) – paired pectoral and pelvic fins; respire by gills; lateral line sense organ; scales.

- ⋆ **Cartilaginous fish** – skeleton of cartilage; no air bladder; e.g. sharks, dogfish.
- ⋆ **Bony fish** – skeleton of bone; air bladder; e.g. trout, herring, etc.

2 **Amphibians** – paired limbs (**tetrapod**) based on pentadactyl plan; aquatic larvae metamorphose into semi-terrestrial adult; adult has simple sac-like lungs; e.g. *Rana* (frog), *Triton* (newt).

3 **Reptiles** – truly terrestrial; scaly skin; lungs are only respiratory surface; shelled eggs with yolk food store; e.g. snakes, lizards, tortoises.

4 **Birds** – closely related to reptiles; adapted to flight.

5 **Mammals** – mammary glands produce milk for young; skin has hair, sweat glands and sebaceous glands; external ear.

Plant kingdom – details

Algae, e.g. Spirogyra

1 **Habitat** – freshwater; floating in still water, e.g. ponds.

2 **Structure** – green; filaments of similar cells, each capable of separate existence; seen as mass of threads.

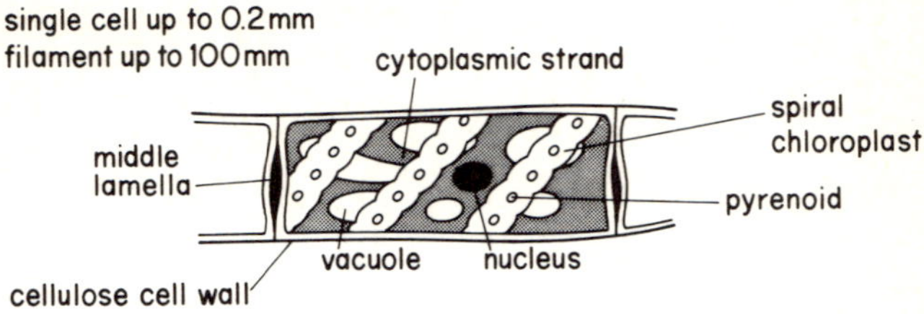

Fig. 15.2 Spirogyra

3 **Nutrition** – photosynthetic; absorbs carbon dioxide and salts from water; starch stored in pyrenoids.

4 **Reproduction.**

- ⋆ **Asexual** – fragmentation; cells divide (binary fission) and filaments increase in length; filaments break up into fragments which grow into new filaments.
- ⋆ **Sexual** – conjugation between two filaments of different strains; often result of overcrowding/adverse conditions.

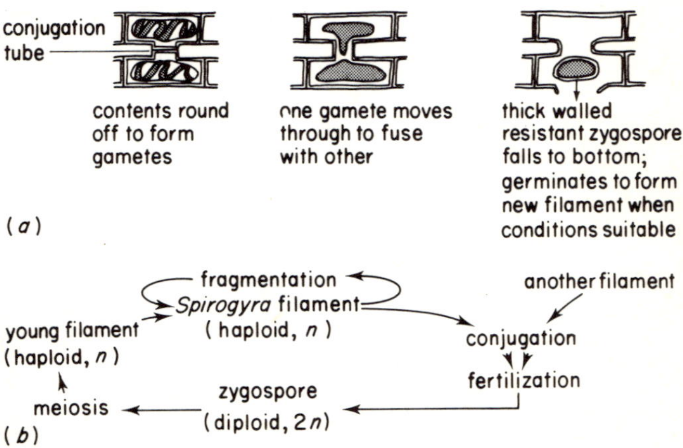

Fig. 15.3 Spirogyra *(a) reproduction (b) life cycle*

Fungi, e.g. **Mucor** ***(pin mould)***

1 **Habitat** – damp dead organic matter, e.g. humus, food.

2 **Structure** – mycelium of branching multinucleate hyphae spreading over dead organic matter.

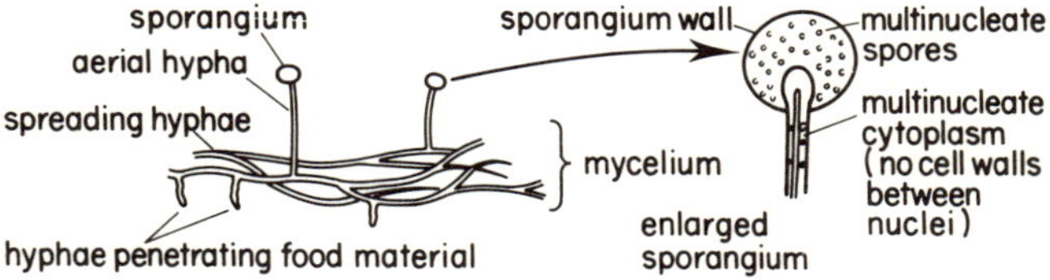

Fig. 15.4 Mucor

3 **Nutrition** – saprophytic; hyphae secrete digestive enzymes onto surface of food, then reabsorb soluble end-products by diffusion over large surface area of hyphae.

4 **Reproduction.**

- **Asexual** – thicker aerial hyphae grow up and swell at tip, producing **sporangium** which produces spores by division of cytoplasm; sporangium absorbs water from aerial hyphae and bursts (**dehisces**); when spores dry they disperse on air currents; if they land on suitable damp material they germinate to form new hyphae.
- **Sexual** – fusion of **gametangia** of different strains growing in contact with each other.

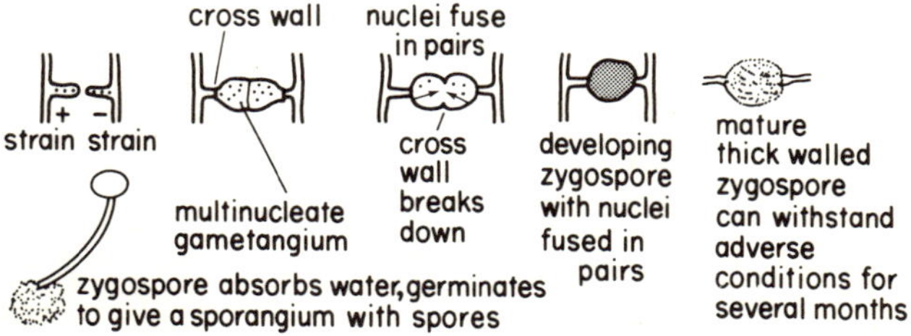

Fig. 15.5 Mucor, *sexual reproduction*

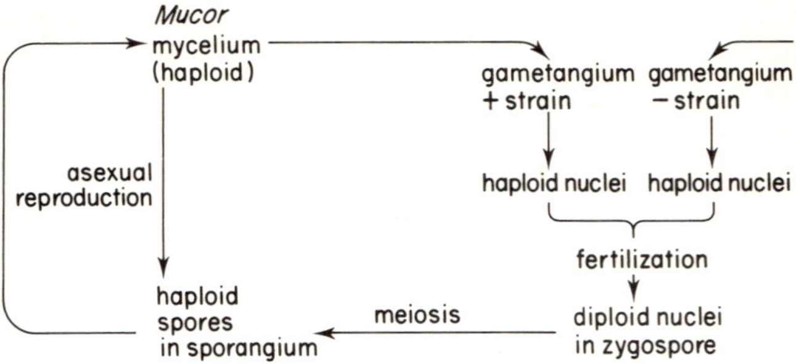

Fig. 15.6 Mucor, *life cycle*

Mosses, e.g.* Funaria *(common moss)

1 **Habitat** – about 2 cm tall; grows in tufts on ground.
2 **Structure** – branched stem; simple oval leaves; no roots but simple multicellular rhizoids; moss plant is **haploid gametophyte generation**; bears sexual reproductive organs (male antheridia, female archegonia) at ends of branches.
3 **Reproduction.**
   - ⋆ **Asexual** – division of plant body.
   - ⋆ **Sexual** – male antheridia produce antherozoids which swim in film of moisture to female archegonia and fertilize female gametes (oospheres); zygote develops into diploid sporogonium (**diploid sporophyte generation**); sporogonium consists of foot, embedded in gametophyte from which it absorbs water and nutrients, seta, which raises capsule, and capsule, which produces **haploid spores by meiosis**; spores released by dehiscent mechanism when dry; spores germinate into thread-like structures (**protonema**) which gives rise to gametophyte plant; life cycle shows **alternation of generations** (see page 113).

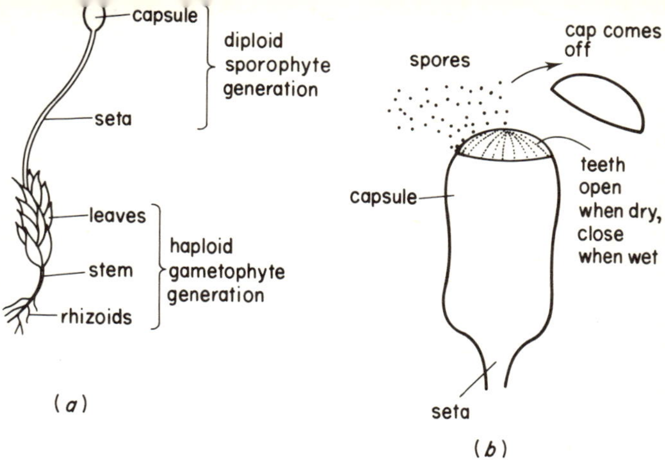

Fig. 15.7 *(a) Moss plant. (b) Spore dispersal*

Ferns, e.g. Dryopteris *(common fern)*

1 **Habitat** – damp shady conditions, e.g. ditches.

2 **Structure** – large leaves (fronds) grow each year from horizontal swollen underground stem (rhizome), die back each winter; special tissues for transport of water and sugars.

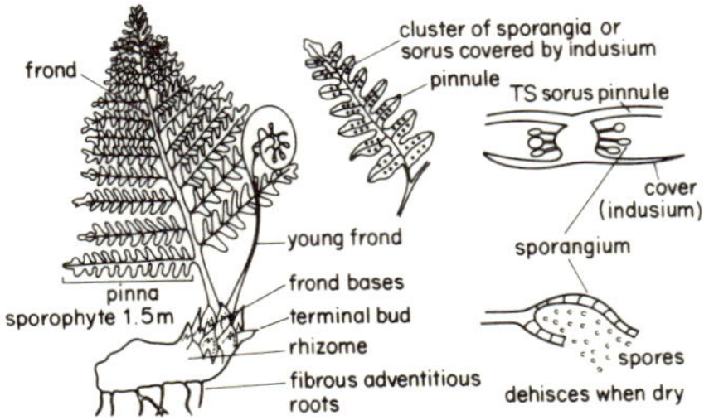

Fig. 15.8 Dryopteris *sporophyte*

3 **Reproduction.**

- ⋆ **Asexual** – underground rhizome branches; branches become detached from rhizome, give rise to new plant.
- ⋆ **Sexual** – the small haploid **gametophyte** prothallus bears sexual reproductive organs; male antheridia produce antherozoids; female archegonia produce oospheres; antherozoids swim in film of moisture to fertilize oospheres; zygote develops into new **sporophyte** fern plant; mature sporophyte fern plant produces **haploid spores by meiosis** on undersurface of certain leaves (**sporophylls**); each haploid spore germinates to give haploid gametophyte plant; life cycle shows **alternation of generations** (see page 113).

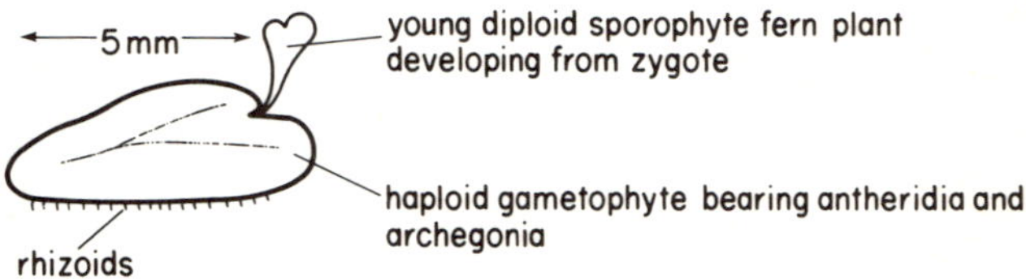

Fig. 15.9 Dryopteris *gametophyte prothallus*

Flowering plants

Flowering plants are the dominant group of terrestrial plants. Many are secondarily aquatic in fresh water, but very few are marine.

1 Flowers are the reproductive structures.
2 Pollen grains contain the male gametes.
3 Ovules in the ovary contain the female gametes.
4 Pollen grains are transported to the stigmas in **pollination**.
5 Male gametes move down the pollen tube to fertilize the female gamete; their movement does not require a film of

water as it does in ferns and mosses. Sexual reproduction in flowering plants is thus better adapted to the terrestrial environment.

6 They produce **seeds** which are enclosed in **fruits**.
7 Tissues are highly differentiated, especially vascular tissue.
8 Flowering plants fall into two main groups:
  * **monocotyledons**;
  * **dicotyledons** – the majority of flowering plants.

Dicotyledons

1 Seeds contain two **cotyledons** (seed leaves).
2 Leaves are typically broad with network pattern of veins.
3 Vascular bundles in the stem are arranged in a circle around the edge.
4 Vascular bundles have a layer of cambium in the centre.
5 Cambium can give rise to secondary thickening to produce woody stems and roots.

Monocotyledons

1 Seeds contain one cotyledon.
2 Leaves are typically long and narrow.
3 Vascular bundles are scattered throughout the stem.
4 Vascular bundles have no cambium.
5 No secondary thickening, so they do not become woody; typically they are herbaceous.
6 Flower parts are usually in threes or multiples of three.
7 Root system typically fibrous, without large central tap-root.

Forms of flowering plants

Flowering plants have a variety of lifespans, from a few weeks to thousands of years.

1 **Ephemerals** flower and set seeds in less than a year; can have two or more generations in one year; no part of plant survives the winter except seeds, which germinate next spring; e.g. groundsel.
2 **Annuals** flower and set seeds once a year; over-winter as seeds; e.g. shepherd's purse, parsley, runner beans.

3 **Biennials** take two years to produce flowers and seeds.
- ⋆ Seed germinates in spring to produce new plant.
- ⋆ Plant grows and stores food (starch or sucrose) in food storage organ (see page 99).
- ⋆ Leaves die in autumn; plant survives winter as swollen underground food storage organ with winter buds.
- ⋆ Next spring plant grows rapidly using stored food; produces leaves, flowers and eventually seeds in summer.
- ⋆ Seeds remain dormant until next spring, when they germinate to produce new plant, e.g. carrot, onion.

4 **Perennials** live and grow for many years, usually producing flowers and seeds every year after a certain age.
- ⋆ **Herbaceous perennials** grow from year to year without producing woody tissues; remain relatively small and herbaceous, e.g. grasses; many have underground food storage organs (bulbs, corms, rhizomes) which carry them over each winter, e.g. daffodil, iris.
- ⋆ **Woody perennials** grow from year to year; develop woody stems and roots.

  Shrubs do not develop main stems or trunk, e.g. gorse.

  Trees develop main stem as trunk, e.g. oak, beech.

  Deciduous shrubs and trees lose leaves in autumn; have buds that remain dormant over winter and which open in spring to produce new shoots and leaves.

  Evergreen shrubs and trees lose leaves irregularly throughout year, so are never without leaves, e.g. pine.

Structure of flowering plants

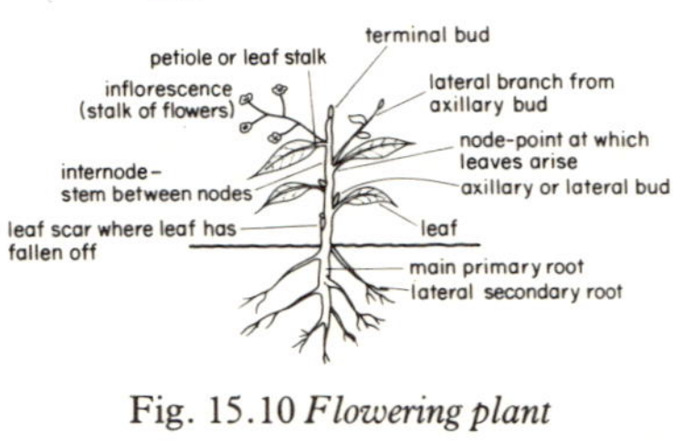

Fig. 15.10 *Flowering plant*

1 **Roots.**
- ⋆ Anchor plant in ground.
- ⋆ Absorb water and mineral ions from soil.
- ⋆ Transport water and mineral ions to stem.
- ⋆ In some plants they store large reserves of food, e.g. dahlia, lesser celandine.

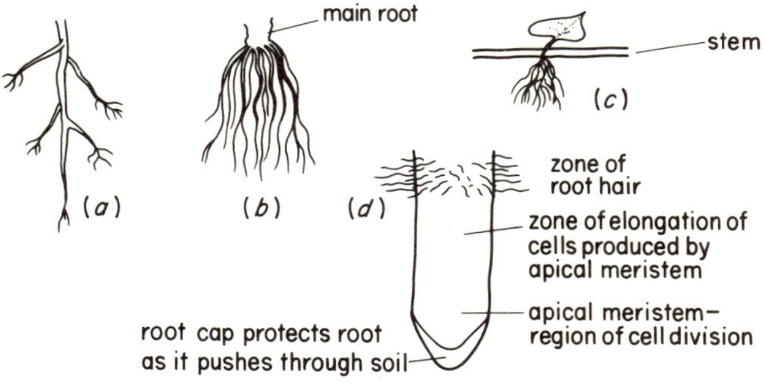

Fig. 15.11 *(a) Tap root. (b) Fibrous roots. (c) Adventitious roots. (d) Detail of root tip*

2 **Leaves.**
- ⋆ Carry out photosynthesis.
- ⋆ Gas exchange for photosynthesis and respiration.
- ⋆ Lose water via transpiration, which draws water and dissolved mineral salts up roots and stems.
- ⋆ In some plants they store large reserves of food, e.g. onion and daffodil bulbs.

3 **Stems.**
- ⋆ Support leaves, exposing them to sunlight for photosynthesis.
- ⋆ Transport water and mineral salts from roots to leaves.

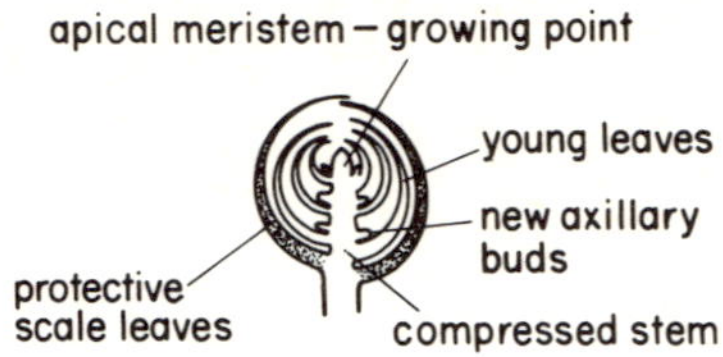

Fig. 15.12 *(a) Stem. (b) LS bud*

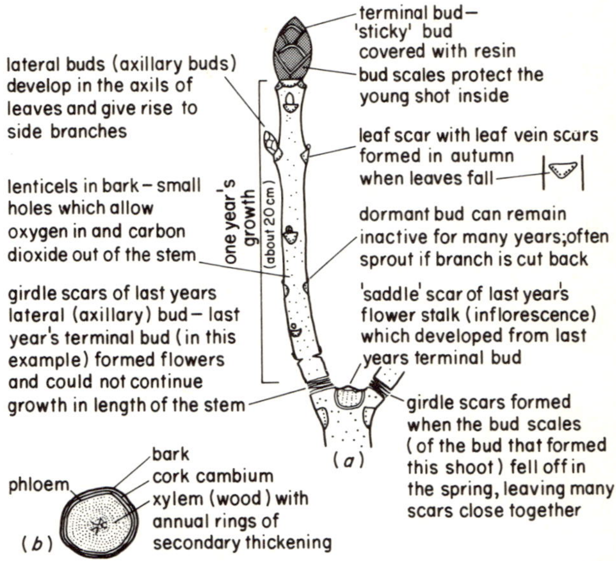

Fig. 15.13 *(a) Horse-chestnut winter twig. (b) TS woody stem*

★ Support leaves in air for gas exchange for photosynthesis and respiration.

* Transport sugars synthesized in leaves by photosynthesis to other non-photosynthetic parts of plant, e.g. roots.
* Modified for food storage in some plants, e.g. potato.

Animal kingdom – details

Protozoa, e.g. Amoeba

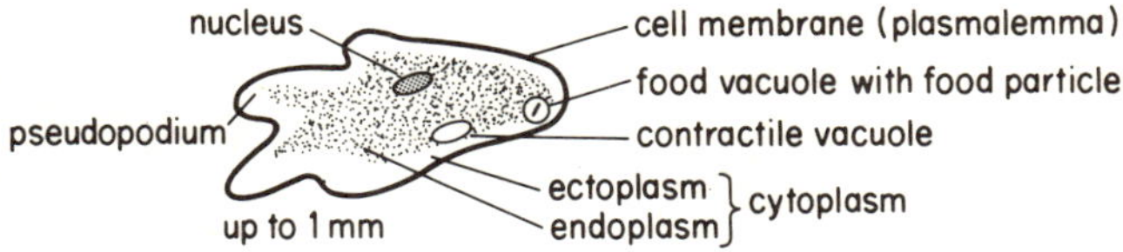

Fig. 15.14 Amoeba

Habitat – freshwater, e.g. ponds.

2 **Movement** – cytoplasm can exist in two states.
* **Plasma-gel** – jelly-like.
* **Plasma-sol** – fluid-like.

Cytoplasm changes between these states, using energy from respiration; as it turns into a sol it flows forward, forming pseudopodia; at front edges it gels again; more sol flows forward from behind.

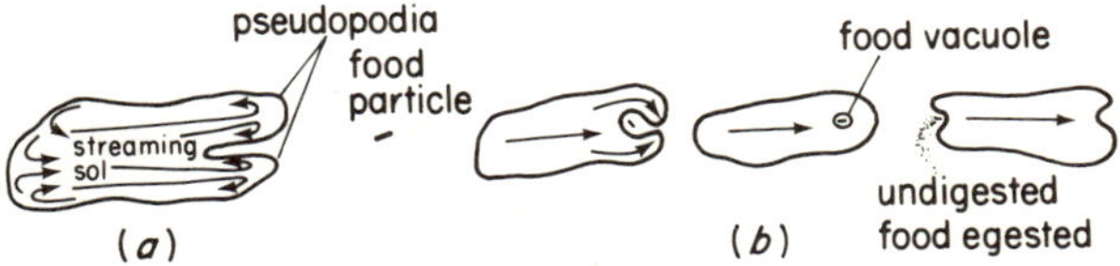

Fig. 15.15 Amoeba *(a) locomotion (b) feeding*

3 **Nutrition.**
* Detects chemicals from food in water (bacteria, diatoms).
* Moves toward food (**positive chemotaxis**).
* Pseudopodia engulf food in vacuole.
* Secretes digestive enzymes into food vacuole.

* Digested food diffuses from vacuole to cytoplasm.
* Undigested food egested by amoeba flowing away from it.

4 **Respiration** – large surface area:volume ratio; diffusion is sufficient for gas exchange.

5 **Osmoregulation** – cytoplasm more concentrated (hypertonic) than freshwater (hypotonic); cell membrane semi-permeable; water continually enters by osmosis; to prevent cell bursting, excess water expelled by contractile vacuole; uses energy from respiration.

6 **Reproduction** – asexual; binary fission; withstands adverse conditions by forming a cyst (**encystment**).

Coelenterates, e.g. Hydra

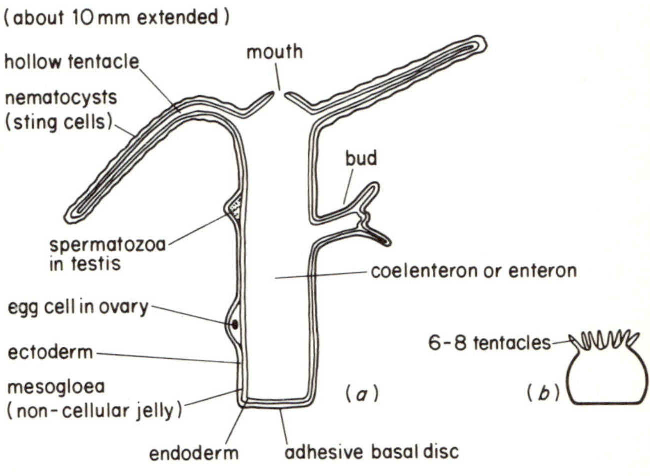

Fig. 15.16 Hydra *(a) LS (b) withdrawn by conctraction of muscles*

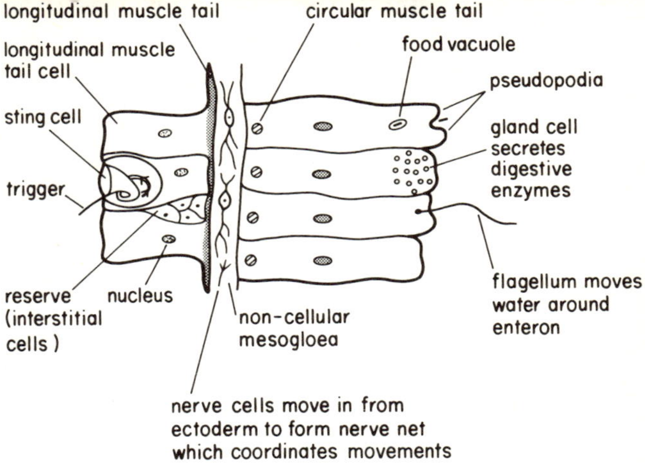

Fig. 15.17 *Detail of section of* Hydra *body wall*

1 **Habitat** – freshwater; usually attached to vegetation.
2 **Movement** – attached to a surface; moves slowly by pulling itself along with its tentacles.
3 **Nutrition** – feeds on small invertebrates, e.g. *Daphnia*.
- Tentacles spread wide; when *Daphnia* comes in contact with tentacle, sting cells (**nematocysts**) are discharged, penetrating and paralyzing prey.
- All tentacles bend towards trapped prey; in coordinated movement push prey into mouth.
- Inside coelenteron, enzymes are secreted onto food by gland cells of endoderm, for extra-cellular digestion.
- Some particles engulfed by pseudopodia of endodermal cells and intra-cellular digestion takes place.
- Soluble end-products of digestion absorbed by diffusion into cytoplasm of cells.
- Undigested food egested via the mouth.

4 **Respiration** – small size, and fact that endodermal cells lining coelenteron are exposed to water entering mouth, results in *Hydra* having large surface area:volume ratio. Diffusion is sufficient for uptake of oxygen, excretion of carbon dioxide and their internal transport. Some species have **symbiotic** algae in their endoderm cells; as a result of photosynthesis these take up carbon dioxide from respiration of *Hydra* cells and give off oxygen, which is used in respiration by *Hydra*.

5 **Reproduction.**

- ⋆ **Asexual** by budding. In favourable conditions *Hydra* develops outgrowths (buds) from body wall by mitotic cell division which develop into small replicas of parent and eventually separate from parent.
- ⋆ **Sexual** by external cross-fertilization. *Hydra* is hermaphrodite, producing both ovaries and testes (seldom produced at same time on one animal). Testes release spermatozoa into the water; they swim to ovary of another animal where one fertilizes an egg. Fertilized egg (zygote) develops into hollow ball of cells inside resistant wall. Protected embryo falls to bottom of the pond; remains dormant until favourable conditions stimulate further development and release of young *Hydra* (which shows genetic variation).

Platyhelminthes, e.g. Taenia solium (pork tapeworm)
Has a number of adaptations to parasitic way of life.

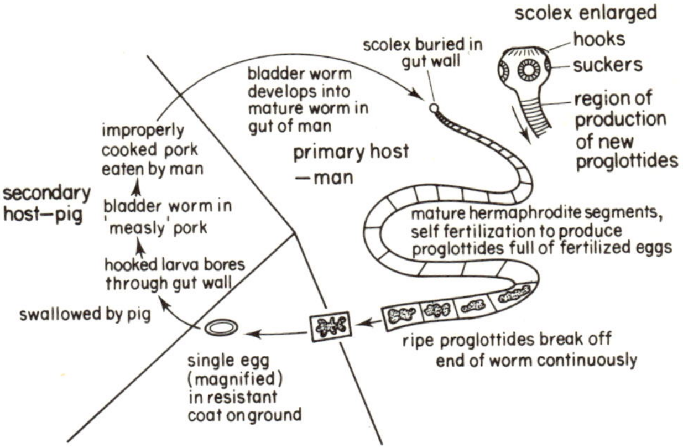

Fig. 15.18 *Pork tapeworm life cycle*

1 Scolex with hooks and suckers to prevent being expelled from gut of host by peristalsis.
2 Thick protective cuticle to resist host's digestive enzymes.
3 Loss or reduction of unnecessary organs.
   - ⋆ No digestive system; digested food absorbed over entire body surface by diffusion.
   - ⋆ Poorly developed muscles and nerves, only capable of weak wriggling movements.
   - ⋆ No major sense organs, as conditions in gut are constant.
4 Large numbers of eggs with resistant coats produced; ensures that some survive to reach secondary host.
5 Complex life history with secondary host; ensures transfer to another primary host.
6 Anaerobic respiration – no oxygen in gut.

Important **methods of control** are as follows.

1 Disposal of human faeces prevents eggs reaching pigs.

2 Inspecting pork for bladder worms ('measly' pork).
3 Cooking pork properly kills any bladder worms.
4 Drugs remove adult worm from gut, although scolex remain to produce new chain of proglottids.

Annelids, e.g. Lumbricus terrestris *(earthworm)*

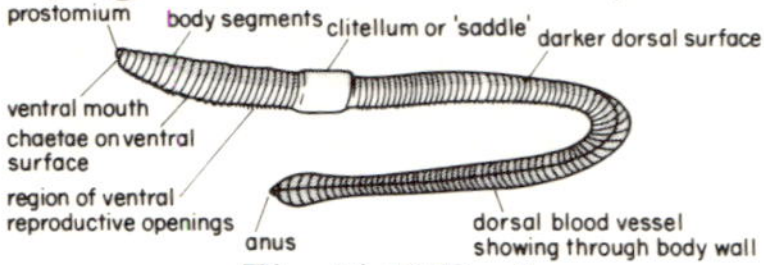

Fig. 15.19 *Earthworm*

1 **Habitat** – burrowing in damp soil.
2 **Movement.**
- ⋆ Circular muscles contract, segments become long and thin.
- ⋆ Longitudinal muscles contract, segments become short and fat.
- ⋆ Waves of contractions pass down body; with action of chaetae, this pushes worm forward through soil.
- ⋆ Emergency 'escape' reaction – whole worm contracts violently back into burrow.

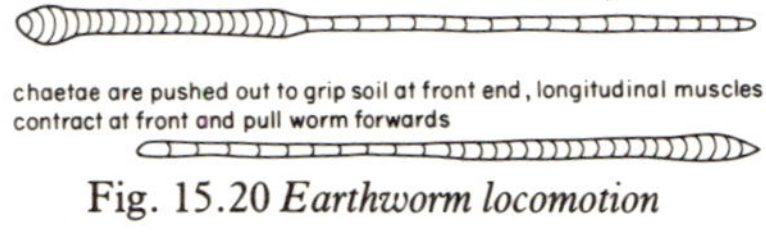

Fig. 15.20 *Earthworm locomotion*

3 **Respiration** – gas exchange (oxygen uptake; carbon dioxide excretion) by diffusion over permeable body surface. Blood contains haemoglobin; combines with oxygen to give oxyhaemoglobin, which is carried to tissues. Thin epidermis with blood capillaries gives problem of water loss (evaporation); to overcome this, gland cells secrete mucus.

4 **Nutrition** – feed on vegetation (leaves) and any organic matter in soil.

- ⋆ Soil containing organic matter is swallowed as worm burrows through soil. Leaves may also be dragged down into burrow and eaten.
- ⋆ Food is ground up in gizzard and passed to region of gut where digestive enzymes are secreted.
- ⋆ Soluble end-products of digestion absorbed by diffusion over large surface area of gut into blood capillaries.
- ⋆ Undigested food is egested via anus. Some worms egest undigested soil as 'worm casts' on surface of soil.

5 **Reproduction** – hermaphrodite; cross-fertilization occurs between two mating worms on soil surface at night.

- ⋆ Worms lie with ventral surface together, head to tail.
- ⋆ Clitellum or 'saddle' of each secretes a band of slime which binds them tightly together.
- ⋆ Spermatozoa are passed from each worm to the other, along grooves, to sperm storage sacs.
- ⋆ Worms separate and return underground.
- ⋆ Clitellum secretes a cocoon which is moved forward around the body like a sleeve.
- ⋆ As it passes over female openings, several eggs are passed in.
- ⋆ As it passes over sperm storage sac openings, spermatozoa (from other worm) are passed in.
- ⋆ Fertilization takes place inside cocoon.
- ⋆ Cocoon containing fertilized eggs is slipped off worm.
- ⋆ After about 12 weeks, one worm emerges (eats others).

6 **Importance in soil fertility.**

- ⋆ Burrows drain, aerate and help break up soil.
- ⋆ Passage of soil through gut breaks it down into fine particles, breaks down organic matter to humus, and makes the soil less acid.
- ⋆ Their waste products and decaying bodies add organic matter.
- ⋆ Soil is 'turned over' by deposit of worm casts above ground.

Arthropods – insects

1 Characteristics.

- ⋆ Body divided into head, thorax and abdomen.
- ⋆ Three pairs of jointed legs attach to thorax.
- ⋆ Two pairs of wings attached to thorax.
- ⋆ Chitin exoskeleton; waterproof surface layer.
- ⋆ One pair of antennae on head.
- ⋆ Respiration by a system of air tubes or trachea.
- ⋆ Life cycles involve moulting (**ecdysis**), metamorphosis.

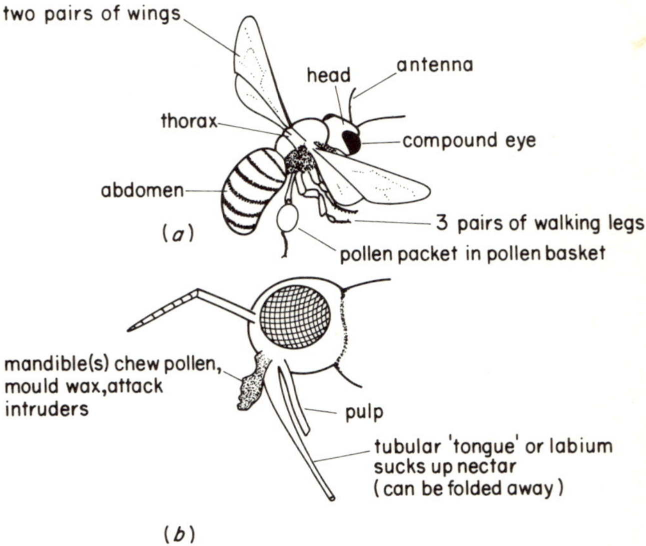

Fig. 15.21 *(a) Honey bee. (b) Honey bee mouthparts*

2 Respiration – controlled openings (**spiracles**) on each segment open into air tubes (**tracheae**) which branch into finer tubes (**tracheoles**) which penetrate individual cells; allow oxygen in air directly to tissues. Tubes are supported by rings of chitin to prevent collapse. At intervals are thin-walled air sacs; act as 'bellows' to ventilate system when squeezed by movements of body. Blood system does *not* transport oxygen.

3 **Insect life cycles** involve **metamorphosis** – juvenile stages change form and develop into adult. As young grow in size they undergo series of moults (**ecdyses**) – exoskeleton shed and body increases rapidly in size before new exoskeleton hardens and restricts growth again.

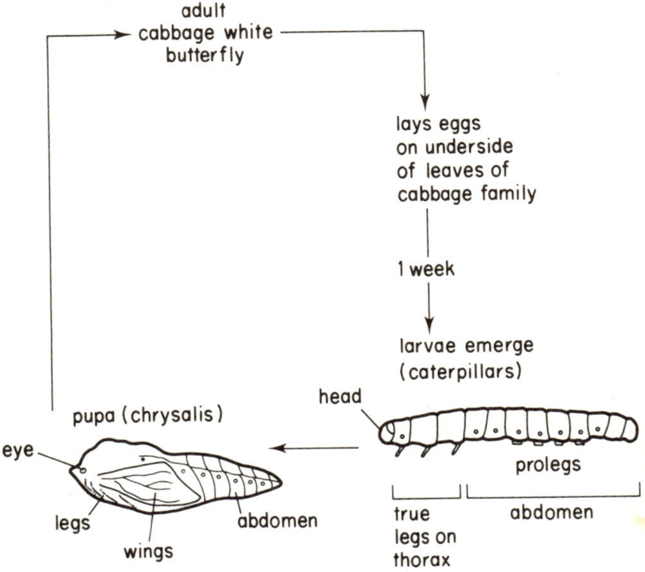

Fig. 15.22 *Cabbage white butterfly, life cycle*

★ **Incomplete metamorphosis** – young (**nymphs**) resemble adults, but lack wings and are sexually immature; nymphs grow, undergo ecdysis several times; each stage between moults called an **instar**; wings develop from external buds visible throughout metamorphosis (**Exopterygota**);

emerge as adult after final moult; e.g. grasshoppers, aphids, cockroaches.

* **Complete metamorphosis** – young (**larvae**) do not resemble adults; typically live in different habitat to adults; larvae grow, undergo ecdysis several times; wings develop from internal buds (**Endopterygota**); forms inactive **pupa** or **chrysalis**; emerge as adult; e.g. moths, butterflies.

Honey bee – life cycle and organization in the community

In summer, colony in hive consists of one egg-laying **queen**, few hundred male **drones** and 20,000–80,000 sterile female **workers**. Queen fed on highly-nutritious **royal jelly** by workers; lays eggs continuously (about 1,500 a day) for the 2–5 years of her life. Queen mates once; stores spermatozoa from drone in sperm-sac; uses throughout her egg-laying life.

1 Queen lays unfertilized and fertilized eggs.
2 Eggs are layed singly in wax cells of comb.
3 Eggs hatch into larvae.
4 Larvae are fed on royal jelly for first three days.
5 Those destined to be queens are only ones that continue to be fed on royal jelly after this period.
6 **Unfertilized eggs** develop into male drones.
   * Drones live for 4–5 weeks.
   * Only role is to fertilize new queen when times comes.
   * Fed by workers – unable to feed themselves.
   * When no longer needed, they are turned out to die.
7 **Fertilized eggs** develop into females. Those fed on royal jelly for more than three days develop into queens.
   * Future queens raised in special queen cells in comb.
   * First queen to emerge destroys other queen.
   * New queen is fertilized by one drone on **nuptial flight**.
   * Before new queen emerges, old queen flies with swarm to found new colony; new queen takes over old colony.
8 Larvae from fertilized eggs fed on royal jelly for three days and then fed on **pollen** and **nectar**; develop into sterile female workers, which have the following tasks.
   * General cleaning of hive.

* Feeding older larvae on nectar and pollen.
* Feeding younger larvae on royal jelly.
* Making wax; building cells of comb.
* Making honey from nectar and pollen; storing it in cells for winter.
* Foraging for food as field bees.
* Guarding hive.

Honey bee differs from other social bees and wasps because the colony exists all year; survive winter on store of honey.

Economic importance of insects

Some insects are **harmful to man**.

1 Cause **damage to crops** by feeding on the plants.
  * **Leaf chewers** with biting mouthparts, e.g. locusts, caterpillars, Colorado beetle larvae on potatoes.
  * **Plant suckers** with piercing and sucking mouthparts, e.g. aphids (greenfly), woolly aphids, root aphids.
  * **Plant borers**, boring through plant tissues, e.g. wireworms (larvae of click-beetles), weevils, sawfly caterpillars, codling moth caterpillars (apple maggots).

2 Cause direct **damage to livestock**.
  * Lice and fleas **suck blood**.
  * Horseflies **bite** viciously.
  * Warble flies **lay eggs** in cattle, etc.; larvae burrow through flesh and skin.

3 Vectors of **plant diseases**.
  * Aphids transmit serious **virus diseases** of crops.
  * Elm bark beetle transmits **Dutch elm disease** fungus.

4 Vectors of **human diseases**.
  * Mosquitoes transmit **malaria** and **yellow fever**.
  * Tse-tse fly transmits **sleeping sickness**.
  * Fleas transmit bubonic **plague** in rats and man.
  * Lice transmit **typhus** fever.

5 Pests of **stored products**.
  * Weevils destroy stored grain.
  * Moth larvae eat wool and destroy clothing.
  * Woodworm beetle larvae bore through wood.

Other insects are **beneficial to man**.

1 **Pollinators** of flowers, e.g. bees and butterflies.
2 **Predators** on insect pests, e.g. ladybirds feed on aphids.
3 **Bees** for honey and wax.
4 **Silkworm** (larvae of a moth) for silk.
5 **Decomposers** of dead organic matter, important in the fertility of the soil, e.g. larvae (maggots) of the flies.

Vertebrates – **Pisces** *(fish), e.g. chub*

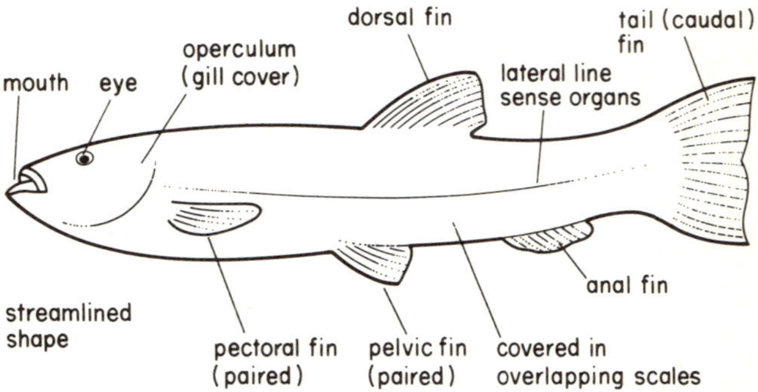

Fig. 15.23 *Fish*

1 **Habitat** – freshwater.
2 **Respiration** – by means of **gills**.
  * Mouth opens, floor of mouth cavity (**pharynx**) lowered.
  * Water drawn in through mouth; **opercula** shut.
  * Mouth closed; floor of mouth raised.
  * Water forced over gills and out through opercula.
  * Gas exchange occurs between water and blood in capillaries of gills: oxygen diffuses from water to blood; carbon dioxide diffuses from blood to water.
  * Gills have: large surface area; delicate lamellae supported by water; thin permeable surface; good supply of blood.
  * Unlike lungs, no danger of desiccation, so no need for mucus layer; diffusion therefore more effective.

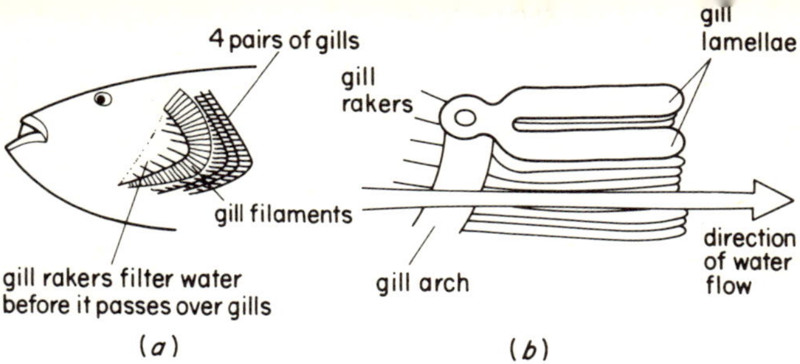

Fig. 15.24 *Fish gills (a) operculum removed (b) TS*

Amphibia, e.g. frog

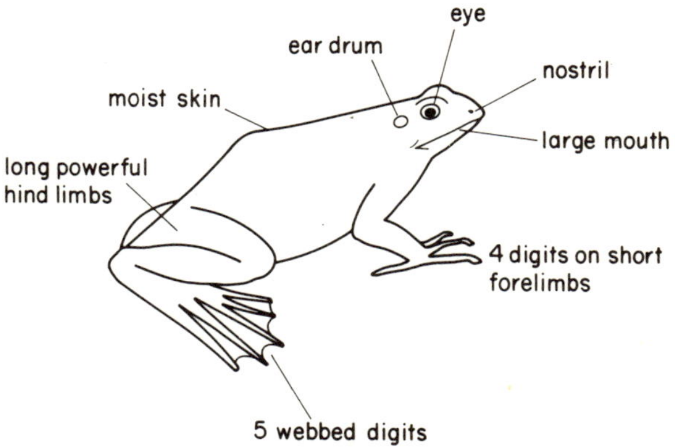

Fig. 15.25 *Frog*

1 **Habitat** – ponds, streams, damp shady places.
2 **Movement.**
   - Powerful hind-limbs for jumping on land.

* Short fore-limbs absorb shock on landing after jumping.
* Powerful hind-limbs and webbed feet for swimming.

3 **Respiration** – the frog has three respiratory surfaces.
* **Skin** is thin, permeable, well supplied with blood capillaries; main respiratory surface in air (oxygen concentration relatively high) and during hibernation.
* **Lungs** are simple, with small surface area; hang in abdomen (no thorax); air pushed in and out by movements of floor of buccal cavity; lungs of importance when frog in water (oxygen concentration relatively low); skin respiration supplemented by air 'gulped' at surface into lungs.
* **Buccal cavity lining** is thin and well supplied with blood vessels; can act as minor respiratory surface.

4 **Nutrition** – carnivorous; feed on insects, insect larvae, earthworms, other small invertebrates; catch prey with long sticky tongue attached at front of buccal cavity (unlike man's).

5 **Reproduction and life history of frog.**
* Mate in water in early spring.
* Male grips female. As eggs are laid, male covers them with seminal fluid containing sperm.
* Fertilization is therefore external.
* Albumen surrounding eggs swells to form frog spawn.
* Each fertilized egg divides by mitosis to form comma-shaped embryo, which feeds on yolk in egg and albumen.
* 2 weeks after fertilization larva (tadpole) emerges; has external gills; feeds on internal yolk; dorsal sucker for attachment to surfaces.
* 3 weeks after fertilization, mouth, coiled gut and anus develop; tadpoles feed on algae; tail elongates.
* 5 weeks after fertilization, respiration by internal gills; hind limb-buds appear; body and tail elongate.
* 7 weeks after fertilization, tadpole becomes carnivorous; fore limb-buds appear; lungs develop.
* 10 weeks after fertilization, limbs continue to develop; tail is reabsorbed; shape begins to be frog-like.
* 12 weeks after fertilization tadpole becomes inactive. Hormones control final metamorphosis into adult; larval skin is shed; all tadpole features disappear; breathes air.

winter they burrow in mud and 'hibernate' in state of torpor, surviving on food stores of fat in body.

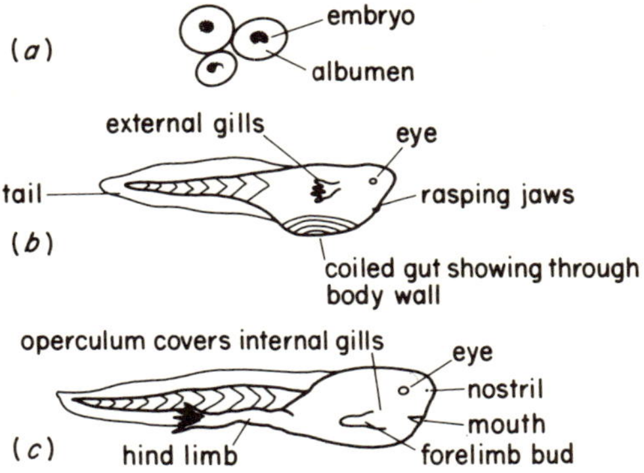

Fig. 15.26 *Frog (a) eggs (b) larval stages*

Birds

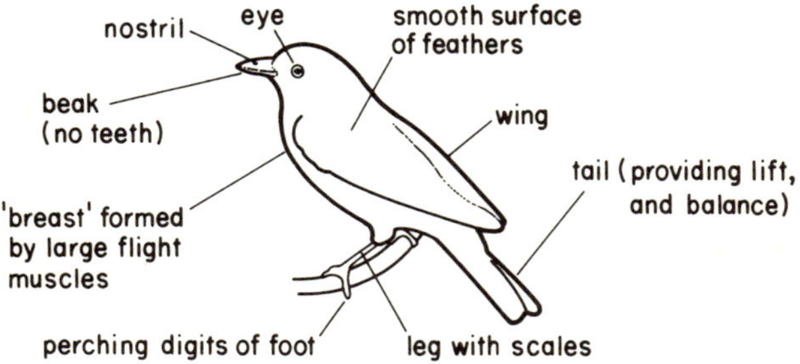

Fig. 15.27 *Bird*

1 Adaptations to flight.

* Fore-limbs form wings; hand and finger bones elongated.
* Feathers give light smooth surface for streamlining; large surface area on wings gives lift. Feathers are also good heat-insulating layer; coloured feathers important in recognition, courtship displays, etc.
* Lungs connected to air sacs in abdomen and in hollow bones; air sacs lighten body.
* Bones hollow, with internal struts; very light and strong.
* Deep breast bone (sternum or keel) to which are attached powerful flight muscles that move wings.

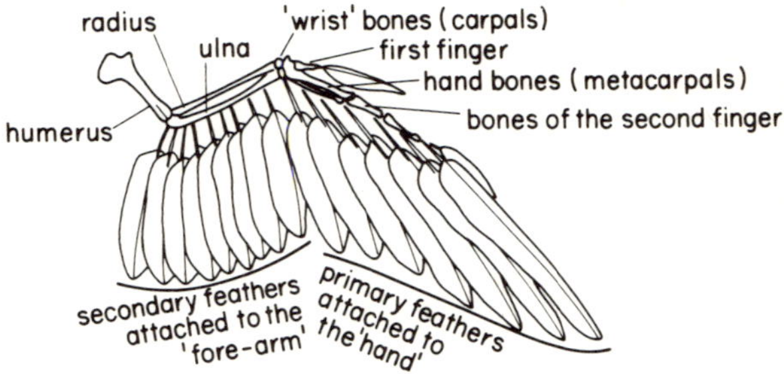

Fig. 15.28 *Bird wing*

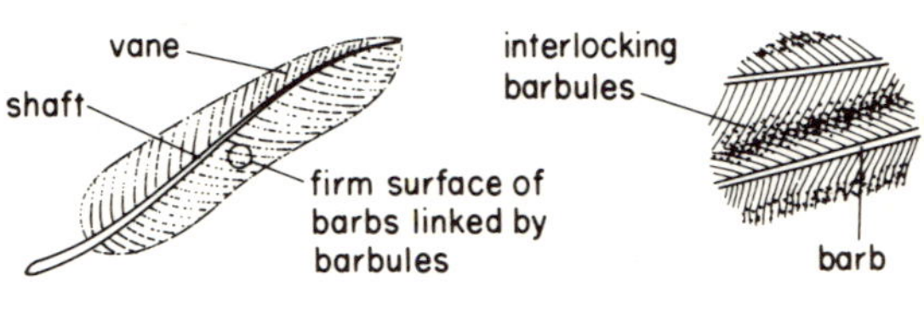

Fig. 15.29 *Bird feather structure*

- ⋆ Often have complex courtship rituals.
- ⋆ Internal fertilization; male deposits sperm in female's oviduct; oviducts lead to cloaca and outside.
- ⋆ Fertilized egg passes down oviduct. Oviduct wall and glands secrete: **yolk** – food store for future embryo; **albumen** – food store, water supply, protection; **shell membranes** – waterproof, prevent loss of water by evaporation through shell; **shell** – calcium carbonate for support, protection, porous to allow gas exchange between embryo and air.
- ⋆ Egg is kept warm (40°C) by parents until hatched.
- ⋆ Chicks need lot of parental care, e.g. feeding, keeping warm, cleaning, protecting, training.

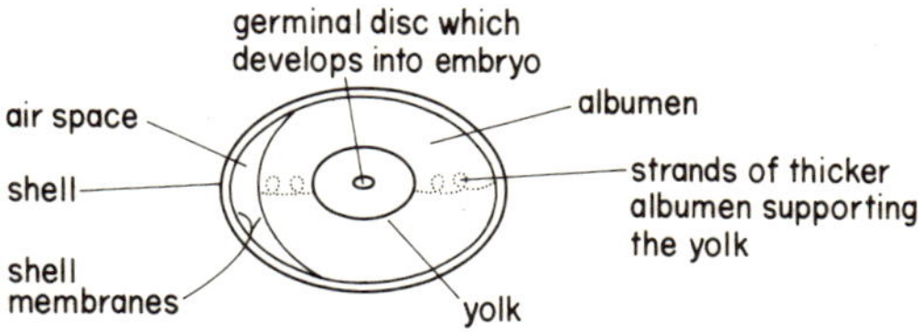

Fig. 15.30 *Bird egg structure*

Comparison of reproduction in fish, frog, bird and mammal

	Fish	*Frog*	*Bird*	*Mammal*
Fertilization	External	External	Internal	Internal
Protection of eggs and embryo	Nest, male fish	Albumen	Nest, shell, parents	Mother's abdomen, amnion, amniotic fluid

	Fish	*Frog*	*Bird*	*Mammal*
Nutrition of embryo	*Yolk*	*Yolk, albumen*	*Yolk, albumen*	*From mother's blood across placenta*
Gas exchange of embryo	*Diffusion with water*	*Diffusion with water*	*Diffusion with air*	*From mother's blood across placenta*
Excretion of embryo	*Diffusion into water*	*Diffusion into water*	*Uric acid crystals in sac*	*Into mother's blood across placenta*

Bacteria

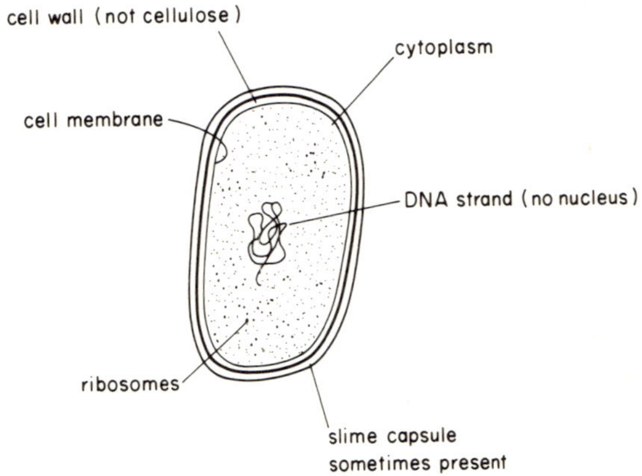

Fig. 15.31 *Bacterium*

1 **Habitat** – virtually all parts of the earth.
2 **Characteristics.**
  - ⋆ Microscopic, unicellular, neither true animals nor plants.
  - ⋆ Size range 0.1 μm–20 μm.

* Four main types: spherical – **cocci**; rod-shaped – **bacilli**; spiral shaped – **spirilla**; curve-shaped – **vibrios**.
* Typically group together in pairs, clusters or chains, e.g. *Staphylococcus* clusters, *Streptococcus* chains.
* On smooth nutrient surface form large visible colonies with characteristic shape, texture and colour by which particular bacteria can be recognized.
* Show wide range of methods of nutrition; most are heterotrophic (saprophytic, parasitic); some are autotrophic (chemosynthetic, photosynthetic).
* Reproduction by binary fission; each cell divides in two. Under good (optimum) conditions this can give rise to a very rapid increase in numbers.
* Of the greatest importance in nature and to man.

Methods of bacterial nutrition and modes of life

1 **Autotrophic.**

* **Photosynthetic bacteria** have a photosynthetic pigment, but it is different from chlorophyll of green plants, and is not enclosed in a chloroplast. Bacterial photosynthesis does *not* evolve oxygen.
* **Chemosynthetic bacteria** make their organic materials from simple inorganic compounds, using energy from inorganic chemical reactions (*not* sunlight as in photosynthesis). Two chemosynthetic bacteria of importance in nitrogen cycle: *Nitrosomonas* obtains energy from conversion of ammonium salts to nitrites; *Nitrobacter* obtains energy from conversion of nitrites to nitrates.

2 **Heterotrophic.**

* **Saprophytic bacteria** live on or in dead organic matter, secreting extracellular digestive enzymes onto it to break it down (hydrolysis) to simple soluble products which are then absorbed over the bacterial surface by diffusion. Dead organic matter is thus decomposed. Along with fungi, they are of great importance in recycling materials in nature and maintaining soil fertility.
* **Symbiotic bacteria** live on or in another organism from which they obtain their food. They also contribute

something useful to the 'host'. Association may be of such importance that one or other cannot survive alone, e.g. bacteria in large intestine of vertebrates, nitrogen-fixing bacteria in root nodules of legumes.

- **Parasitic bacteria** live on or in another organism from which they obtain their food. Cause diseases of plants and animals by destroying cells and tissues, and by excreting poisons (toxins) which disrupt host's metabolism, thus producing disease symptoms.

Bacterial disease

Parasitic bacteria that penetrate the body's defences against disease and multiply sufficiently cause the disease symptoms. A widespread outbreak in a population is an **epidemic**.

1 **Methods of infection.**
   - **Direct contact** with infected person, particularly via broken skin or membranes, e.g. lining of mouth, reproductive organs.
   - **Indirect contact** via infected object.
   - **Droplet infection** – inhaling droplets of moisture from infected person coughing, sneezing, spitting, etc.
   - Swallowing **infected food** or **water**, e.g. typhoid, cholera.
   - **Direct entry** via cuts (not from an infected person or object), e.g. tetanus in the soil entering a wound.
   - **Vector bites**, e.g. malaria transmitted by mosquitoes.

2 **Defences against infection.**
   - **Skin** forms a defensive barrier.
   - **Mucus** secretion traps disease organisms.
   - **Immune system** and vaccination (see page 47).
   - Knowledge and behaviour, e.g. exercising **hygiene**.

3 **Prevention of infection.**
   - **Isolation** of infected people.
   - Isolation, and sometimes **destruction**, of infected animals.
   - General **hygiene** and cleanliness, including: personal hygiene; food hygiene; food preservation, including refrigeration; water purification; sewage treatment and refuse disposal.

Legislation, e.g. notification of outbreaks, control of movements of people and animals from infected areas.
* **Treatment** of infected people: general medical care; injection of ready made antibodies; antibiotics, produced by fungi, e.g. penicillin, or artificially, destroy bacteria (*not* viruses).

Viruses

Viruses are neither plants nor animals, nor do they show all the characteristics of living things.

1. Much smaller than bacteria; cannot be seen under the light microscope.
2. Can only be seen under electron microscope (magnifies many hundred times more than light microscope).
3. Consist of a protein coat surrounding nucleic acid (either RNA or DNA) which is the genetic material.
4. Invade cells (of a host) by injecting nucleic acid into them. The nucleic acid then 'instructs' the host cell to make new virus particles. Eventually the host cell ruptures and new virus particles are released to invade other host cells.
5. They thus destroy host cells, causing disease.
6. Viral diseases in man include smallpox, polio, influenza, common cold, German measles.
7. Plant virus diseases include potato leaf roll virus, leaf mosaic virus.
8. Virus diseases of man are resisted by the same methods as for bacterial diseases, plus interferon – a special substance produced by cells.

Size scales

Metre	*Millimetre*	*Micrometre*	*Nanometre*	
10^{-3}m	**1 mm**	1,000 μm	1,000,000 nm	*Amoeba*
10^{-4}m	0.1 mm	100 μm	100,000 nm	
10^{-5}m	0.01 mm	10 μm	10,000 nm	RBC (7 μm)
10^{-6}m	0.001 mm	**1 μm**	1,000 nm	
10^{-7}m	0.0001 mm	0.1 μm	100 nm	Limit of light microscope

Metre	*Milli-metre*	*Micro-metre*	*Nano-metre*	
10^{-8}*m*	*0.00001 mm*	*0.01 µm*	*10 nm*	*Viruses, cell organelles, large molecules*

Use of simple keys to identify organisms

Simple keys are used to identify different organisms. Observable features are used to separate organisms into smaller and smaller groups, until the animal or plant can be identified on the basis of features that it alone possesses.

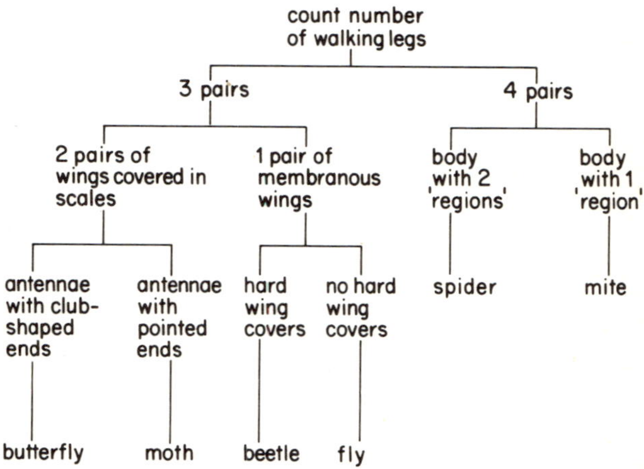

Fig. 15.32 *Simple key to identify some invertebrates*

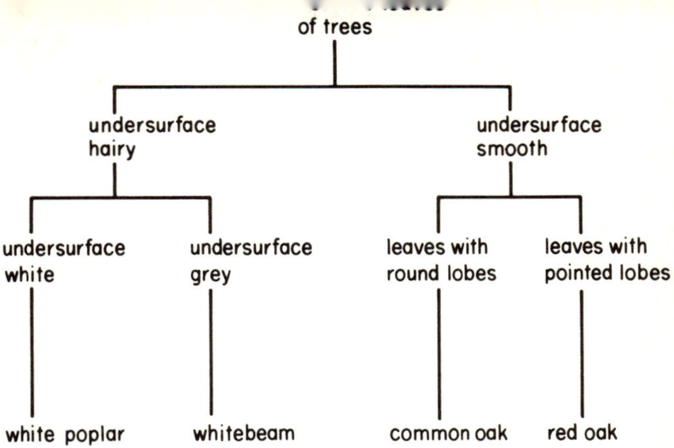

Fig. 15.33 *Simple key to identify some plants*

Notes

Notes

Notes